United Nations Conference on Trade and Development

Investment Policy Review

Republic of Belarus

UNITED NATIONS
New York and Geneva, 2009

NOTE

UNCTAD serves as the focal point in the United Nations Secretariat within its mandate on trade and development for all matters related to foreign direct investment, as part of its work on trade and development. This function was formerly performed by the United Nations Centre on Transnational Corporations (UNCTC) (1975–1992). UNCTAD's work is carried out through intergovernmental deliberations, research and analysis, technical assistance activities, seminars, workshops and conferences.

The term "country" as used in this study also refers, as appropriate, to territories or areas; the designations employed and the presentation of the material do not imply the expression of any opinion whatsoever on the part of the Secretariat of the United Nations concerning the legal status of any country, territory, city or area or of its authorities, or concerning the delimitation of its frontiers or boundaries. In addition, the designations of country groups are intended solely for statistical or analytical convenience and do not necessarily express a judgement about the stage of development reached by a particular country or area in the development process.

The following symbols have been used in the tables:

Two dots (..) indicate that data are not available or not separately reported. Rows in tables have been omitted in those cases where no data are available for any of the elements in the row.

A hyphen (-) indicates that the item is equal to zero or its value is negligible.

A blank in a table indicates that the item is not applicable.

A slash (/) between dates representing years – for example, 2004/05 – indicates a financial year.

Use of a dash (–) between dates representing years – for example, 2004–2005 – signifies the full period involved, including the beginning and end years.

Reference to "dollars" ($) means United States dollars, unless otherwise indicated.

Annual rates of growth or change, unless otherwise stated, refer to annual compound rates.

Details and percentages in tables do not necessarily add to totals because of rounding.

The material contained in this study may be freely quoted with appropriate acknowledgement.

UNCTAD/DIAE/PCB/2009/10

UNITED NATIONS PUBLICATION
Sales No. E.09.II.D.19
ISBN 978-92-1-112780-5

PREFACE

The UNCTAD Investment Policy Reviews (IPRs) are intended to help countries improve their investment policies and to familiarize governments and the international private sector with an individual country's investment environment. The reviews are considered by the UNCTAD Commission on Investment and Enterprise Development.

The Investment Policy Review of Belarus, initiated at the request of the Belarusian Government, was carried out through a fact-finding mission in May 2008, and is based on information current at that date and additional information made available to UNCTAD until 30 April 2009. The mission received the full cooperation of the relevant ministries and agencies, in particular the Ministry of Economy and the National Investment Agency. The mission also benefited from the views of the private sector, foreign and domestic, and the resident international community, particularly bilateral donors and development agencies. A preliminary version of this report was discussed with stakeholders at a national workshop in Minsk on 8 April 2009. The final report reflects written comments from various ministries of the Government of Belarus.

The suitability and effectiveness of the regulatory regime is assessed against several related criteria: (a) whether the regulation adequately promotes and protects the public interest; (b) whether the regulation adequately promotes investment and sustainable socio-economic development; and (c) whether the policies employed are effective and well administered, given their public interest and development objectives and the legitimate concerns of investors that rules and procedures do not unduly burden their competitiveness. International practices are taken into account in making the assessment and recommendations in this report.

In addition to reviewing the investment framework, the report elaborates on a strategy to maximize the positive impact of foreign direct investment (FDI) on the development of the local small and medium-sized enterprise (SME) sector. This follows a specific request from the Government of Belarus to focus on this sector.

The report was prepared by the Investment Policy Reviews Section under the direction of Chantal Dupasquier and the supervision of James Zhan. It was written by Paige Griffin, Massimo Meloni, Antal Szabo, Elisabeth Turner and Peter Zashev. Substantive contributions from Rory Allan, Hamed El Kady, Maryam Gilmitdinova, Anna Joubin-Bret and Violeta Mitova are also acknowledged. The report benefited from comments and suggestions from UNCTAD colleagues under a peer review process. Lang Dinh provided research assistance and Elisabeth Anodeau-Mareschal provided production support. This report was funded by the United Nations Development Programme (UNDP) office in Belarus, which also provided logistical support. Antonius Broek, the Resident Representative and his team collaborated closely with UNCTAD throughout the preparation of the IPR.

It is hoped that the analysis and recommendations will contribute to improved policies, promote dialogue among stakeholders, catalyse investment and the beneficial impact of FDI and ultimately help the Government of the Republic of Belarus achieve its development objectives.

Geneva, July 2009

CONTENTS

FIGURES

BOXES

ABBREVIATIONS

BYR	Belarusian rouble
BIT	bilateral investment treaty
CIS	Commonwealth of Independent States
DTT	double taxation treaty
EBRD	European Bank for Reconstruction and Development
EU	European Union
EurAsEC	Eurasian Economic Community
FDI	foreign direct investment
FEZ	free economic zone
GDP	gross domestic product
GSP	generalized system of preferences
ICC	International Chamber of Commerce
ICSID	International Convention for the Settlement of Investment Disputes
IFC	International Finance Corporation
ILO	International Labour Organization
IMF	International Monetary Fund
IPA	investment promotion agency
IPR	Investment Policy Review
IT	Information technology
LIBOR	London Interbank Offered Rate
M&A	mergers and acquisitions
NIPC	National Intellectual Property Centre
OAO	open joint-stock company
OOO	limited liability company
PPP	public-private partnership
SME	small and medium-sized enterprise
SOE	state-owned enterprise
TNC	transnational corporation
TRIPS	Trade-Related Aspects of Intellectual Property Rights
UNCITRAL	United Nations Commission on International Trade Law
UNDP	United Nations Development Programme
VAT	value added tax
WIPO	World Intellectual Property Organization
WTO	World Trade Organization
ZAO	closed joint-stock company

BELARUS

Doing business 2010

	Belarus	Latvia	South Africa	Eastern Europe and Central Asia Average
Starting a business (# of days)	6	16	22	6.7
Cost of registering property (per cent of property value)	0	2	8.7	2.2
Investor protection index	4.7	5.7	8	5.5
Rigidity of employment index	11	43	35	29.2
Difficulty of redundancy Index	20	50	30	25.9
Difficulty of hiring Index	0	40	56	31.9
Redundancy cost (weeks of wages)	22	17	24	26.6
Cost of enforcing contracts (per cent of claim)	23.4	23.1	33.2	25.6
Time to exports (days)	16	13	30	26.8
Time to import (days)	21	12	35	11

BELARUS	1990-99 average	2000-05 average	2006	CIS average or total (2006)
Key economic and social indicators				
Population (millions)	10.2	9.9	9.7	277.4
GDP at market prices (billion dollars)	15.4	18.5	36.9	1,282
GDP per capita (dollars)	1,511.6	1,867.2	3,796.1	4,621.5
Real GDP growth (per cent)	-1.6	7.3	9.9	7.5
Poverty rate (percentage living under $1/day)	..	..	..	..
GDP by sector (per cent):				
Agriculture	18	11.4	9.3	6
Industry	41.6	39.1	42	39
Services	40.4	49.5	48.7	54.2
Trade (millions of dollars):				
Merchandise exports	5,540.8	10,416.1	19,738.5	425,589.1
Services exports	629.7	1,448.3	2,299.2	52,570
Merchandise imports	6,580.2	11,796.9	22,323.2	281,507.5
Services imports	314.6	922.5	1,486.9	69,654.5
Capital flows (millions of dollars):				
Net FDI flows	144.1	183.7	354	42,934.5
Net flows from private creditors	76.8	-41.2	30	-4,547.6
Net flows from official creditors	79	24.8	1.1	-25,829.1
Grants	107.2	..	76.2	1,977.5
Life expectancy at birth (years)	69.1	68.4	68.6	68
Export of goods and services (per cent of GDP)	55.5	65.4	59.9	37.7
Import of goods and services (per cent of GDP)	59.8	68.7	64.2	27.4
FDI inflows (per cent of GDP)	1.1	1.1	1	3.4
Infant mortality rate (per thousand)	19.2	13.6	11.8	32.1
Literacy rate, adult (per cent)	99.6	..	..	..
Literacy rate, youth (per cent)	99.8	..	..	..

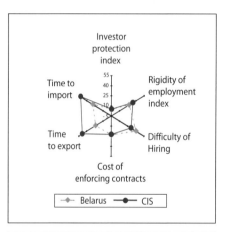

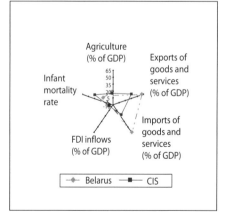

Sources: UNCTAD, FDI/TNC database, World Bank (Doing Business 2007&2008) World Development Indicators and Global Development Finance. UNDP, Human Development Report 2007/2008

INTRODUCTION

The Republic of Belarus is a member of the Commonwealth of Independent States (CIS), formed in 1991 at the dissolution of the Soviet Union. Following an initial transition period characterized by a sharp decline in its gross domestic product (GDP), the country has experienced solid economic growth, while maintaining the key features of a planned economy. This good performance was favoured by substantial subsidies derived from preferential prices on energy (oil and gas) and trade preferences granted by the Russian Federation. In light of a new agreement initiated by the Russian Federation on energy prices, some of these advantages are scheduled to gradually disappear. Thus, by 2011, energy prices paid by Belarusian importers would be at par with world prices. At the same time, the international economic crisis is taking a heavy toll on Belarusian exports and GDP growth.

In order to address these changes and better face an increasingly competitive world economy, the government is seeking new ways to support growth and the economic development of the country, including by fostering private investment, both domestic and foreign. Against this background, the authorities have undertaken, since 2007, a series of ambitious measures aimed at liberalizing the economy and promoting the development of the private sector. Indeed, while the country depends heavily on state-owned enterprises (SOEs), the overall environment for private sector development had for long been neglected. Characterized by heavy regulations and administrative procedures, Belarus had not attracted many foreign investors.

The government's commitment to reform will be an important factor in delivering further improvements. In this context, this investment policy review seeks to identify a number of areas where determined and coordinated action would enhance the competitiveness of the public and private sectors in Belarus and increase the country's attractiveness as an investment location. FDI can play a strategic role in facilitating the transition process and integrating the country into the global economy. Belarus' unexploited FDI potential is large and can be fully tapped only if issues such as competition, private sector development and credibility regarding business-friendly reforms are adequately addressed. At the same time, a number of reforms are needed if FDI is to contribute to the development of the Belarusian economy, in particular the local SME sector, which is the strategic focus of this report, at the request of the government.

The report is structured as follows. Chapter I presents an overview of FDI trends and impact, following a brief economic background. While Belarus benefits from good infrastructure, a highly skilled labour force and a privileged location between the Russian Federation and Western Europe, the country has so far failed to attract large inflows of FDI. Indeed, in comparison to other CIS countries and similar transition economies, Belarus has performed relatively poorly. In this context, the impact of FDI on the local economy has been limited, with the exception of those sectors with a significant FDI presence, such as telecommunications and banking.

Chapter II reviews and assesses the investment framework. While the country is generally open to FDI, it was only in 2007 that the government seriously committed to significantly improve its investment climate and make FDI attraction a key policy objective. Since then, an impressive number of reforms have been undertaken with a view to addressing regulatory impediments, improving the interface between the public and private sectors and reducing the cost of doing business. However, the excessive regulation of business activity, a weak competition regime and the persistence of heavy wage and price controls still inhibit private sector development. Moreover, issues remain in the implementation of the recent reforms by the administrative machinery.

Chapter III outlines a strategy to support SME development through FDI. Notwithstanding existing policies and institutions to foster SME development, the sector's contribution to total GDP and employment remains very low, and SMEs are not integrated into the supply chains of local and foreign investors. The ability of SMEs to reap the benefits from foreign investment therefore remains very limited. FDI can and should be better utilized to contribute to the development of this sector, but to reach this end, a more decisive stance towards reducing the constraints to SME development as well as more targeted policy initiatives are needed.

Chapter IV summarizes the key findings of the review and presents the main recommendations.

CHAPTER I

FDI TRENDS AND PERFORMANCE

Over the last decade, Belarus has experienced an unprecedented period of growth while maintaining an economic model based on state planning and state enterprises. The continued sustainability of this growth is increasingly being challenged by the effects of the global economic crisis of 2008–2009 and the comparative rise in energy prices due to the gradual elimination of subsidies and their eventual alignment to world market prices. FDI inflows have traditionally been very low, discouraged by frequent policy changes and an ambiguous policy stance towards private sector development.

Since late 2007, in an effort to maintain high levels of economic growth, Belarus has launched reforms to develop the private sector, which currently accounts for only around 25 per cent of GDP. In this context, ambitious goals have also been set to increase FDI inflows from 2.6 per cent to 15–20 per cent of total investment (Foreign Investment Consultative Council of the Council of Ministers of Belarus, 2008) and to move into the top 25 countries in the World Bank's "Doing Business" rankings.

A very large number of policy changes affecting both domestic and foreign investment have followed and many more are envisaged. The absence of a visible and publicly discussed private sector development strategy, however, risks jeopardizing the effectiveness of the efforts underway. The extent to which FDI inflows to Belarus will react to these changes in a sustained way will also depend on the ability of policymakers to convey a coherent and consistent message not only to international investors but also to the internal administration in charge of day-to-day policy implementation.

A. Economic background

In 1991, the newly independent states formed as a result of the dissolution of the Soviet Union began independent economic policymaking.[1] The majority of the CIS countries[2] pursued liberalization and privatization. In contrast, Belarus chose to maintain a centrally planned economy with limited forays into privatization. Belarus' socially oriented economic policy[3] has continued to preserve the main elements of that policy approach through the present, with the general result of a dominant state presence in agriculture, industry and services, a limited private sector and low FDI inflows.

In the years immediately following independence, Belarus' economy was contracting and inflation was uncontrolled. Five years after independence, GDP per capita had declined to a third of its 1991 level. After elections in 1994, the government pursued a new growth strategy and adopted expansionary credit policies combined with strict wage, price and output controls. It also favoured extensive state support of industry and agriculture, which frequently involved interventions in credit decisions by the central bank.

Initially, the growth strategy had positive effects. It stimulated employment and domestic consumption and, to an extent, mitigated the effects of the dissolution of the Soviet Union. The economy began growing and GDP per capita returned to pre-independence levels. But this proved to be an unsustainable strategy. Inflation, which had declined dramatically from 2,000 per cent in 1994 to 53 per cent in 1996, began to climb again, reaching over 200 per cent in 1999.

---

[1] Although 1991 was the official year of independence for Belarus, it was not until 1994 that a national constitution was adopted and a President was elected to replace the office of Prime Minister.

[2] Initially consisting of 11 former members of the Soviet Union, today there are nine full members: Armenia, Azerbaijan, Belarus, Kazakhstan, Kyrgyzstan, the Republic of Moldova, the Russian Federation, Tajikistan and Uzbekistan. Turkmenistan discontinued permanent membership as of 26 August 2005 and is now an associate member. Georgia announced its withdrawal in August 2008. Ukraine is not a member but participates in several agreements.

[3] "Socially oriented" is the term used to describe the approach to economic planning in Belarus.

Figure I.I. Real GDP growth and inflation 1993–2007

(Annual average in per cent)

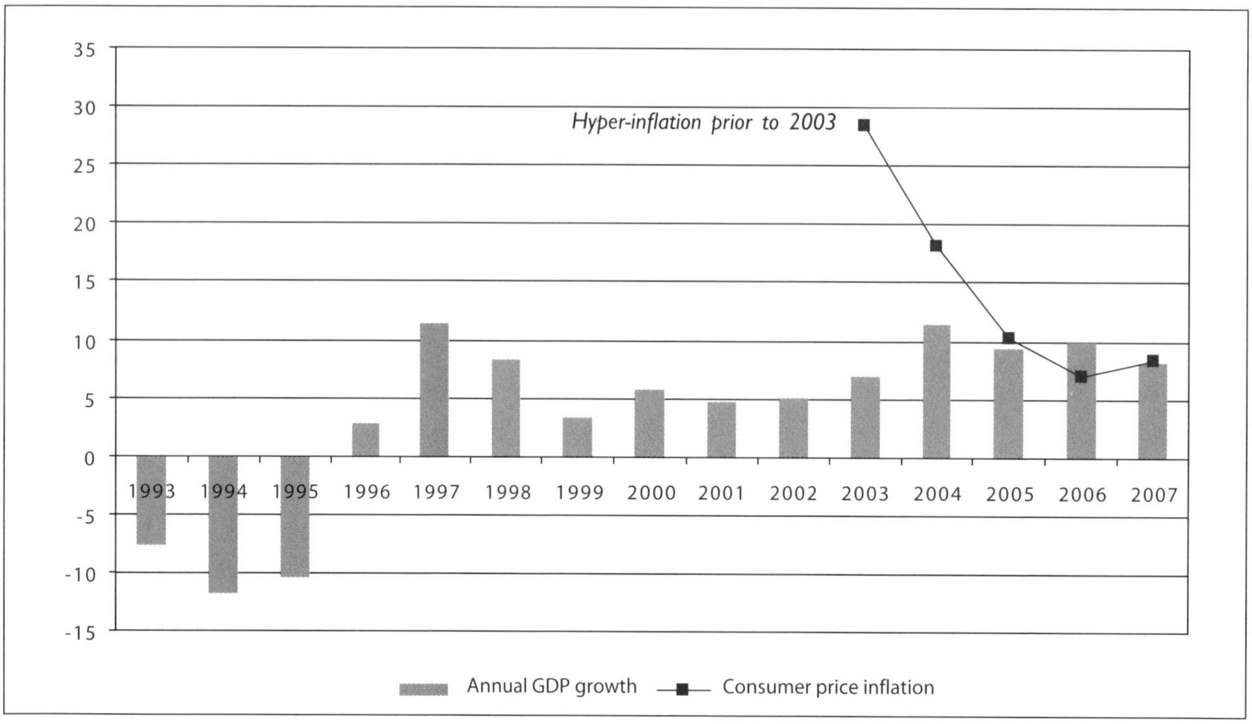

Source: World Bank Database.

In 2000, the government began restoring macroeconomic order and bringing inflation under control by tightening monetary policy – increasing lending rates and limiting government interventions in credit allocation. It also began moving away from the barter system that had arisen with the Russian Federation,[4] improved central budget management (following international accounting standards) and consolidated an unwieldy budget.[5] The multiple exchange rate system maintained since the early transition years was unified. The economy responded to the policy changes and grew at a fairly rapid pace, remaining above 8 per cent from 2004 to the present (figure I.I).

External factors were also at work driving economic growth in Belarus. During the initial period of independence, Belarus worked aggressively to rebuild trade with the Russian Federation. Through the arrangements negotiated during this time, Belarus was able to preserve the preferential oil and gas import pricing it enjoyed in the Soviet era and to secure advantageous market access for its products. This gave Belarus the ability to earn significant revenues from the re-export of oil and gas.[6] For example, by 2004, Belarus was purchasing gas from the Russian Federation at $48 per 1,000 cubic meters while Western Europe was paying $135. Similarly, Belarus paid $25 per barrel of oil compared to the international price of $37.[7] Cheap energy, preferential access to the Russian market and a lower wage rate made Belarusian exports to the Russian Federation very competitive. Concurrently, the Russian Federation's economic growth fuelled demand for the cheaper Belarusian goods.

---

[4]   In 1993, 24 per cent of Belarusian exports and 23 per cent of imports were in the form of barter. This grew to 35.5 per cent by 2000 (Robinson, 2004).

[5]   Improvements included the adoption of a comprehensive legal and administrative framework for fiscal management, budget consolidation, the incorporation of off-budget funds and the expansion of treasury coverage to include local and regional budgets (World Bank, 2005).

[6]   Exports of oil products reached about 13 million tons in 2004, about two thirds of the total output (ibid.).

[7]   Figures cited were originally provided in tons, $181 per ton and $275 per ton respectively (ibid.).

The rapid pace of economic growth has slackened somewhat since 2006, declining from 10 to 8 per cent. The 2007 increase in oil and gas prices following a new energy agreement with the Russian Federation is an important factor explaining the slowdown, as 97 per cent of power production in Belarus is based on gas, the majority of which is supplied by the Russian Federation. The agreement signed in 2007 allows the Russian Federation to steadily raise the price of gas and oil exports to Belarus until 2011, at which time they are set to converge with world market prices.[8] However, in 2007, the rise in the price of energy imports to Belarus (14 per cent)[9] was more than offset by the rise in the international prices for oil and gas. This enabled the government to continue subsidizing domestic exporters, largely SOEs.

Since then, oil and gas prices have significantly declined, in reaction to the global economic crisis that started in 2008. Eventually, however, energy prices in Belarus will be aligned to the market prices. The more expensive gas imports reduce the government's margin on gas re-exports while increasing the cost of subsidizing domestic consumption and industry.[10] This could be particularly challenging at a time when wage increases are hindering price competitiveness (World Bank, 2005). Also, Belarusian exports are declining due to the global economic slowdown, which pushed the authorities to devalue the Belarusian rouble by 20 per cent in January 2009. These issues are exacerbated by the dominant role of SOEs in economic production, along with the continued reliance on price controls and subsidies, which limit internal competition. To address these challenges, government initiatives are underway to diversify away from gas and into wind and water resources as possible alternative energy sources, including by means of attracting FDI in these areas.[11]

Hence the pressing need for an infusion of fresh investment, both domestic and foreign, to modernize the economy and take advantage of Belarus' competitive assets including its privileged geographical position between the Russian Federation and the European Union (EU) as well as its transport infrastructure and highly skilled labour force.

At the same time, Belarus started the process of accession to the World Trade Organization (WTO) (box 1.1), which will require economic liberalization in various sectors. Against this background, Belarus has begun to consider the advantages of divesting its SOEs and creating new opportunities for local and foreign investors.

---

[8] The agreement also stipulates that the Russian enterprise Gazprom will be allowed to purchase shares of Beltranzgaz (Belarus) each year until Gazprom has 50 per cent ownership.

[9] Ministry of Economy, meeting with UNCTAD on 12 May 2008.

[10] Subsidies on products as a per cent of GDP were increasing (3.8 per cent in 2002 to 5.4 per cent in 2006) prior to the new gas and oil agreement with the Russian Federation (Ministry of Statistics and Analysis (MSA), 2007). The figures only reflect direct budget support; therefore it is likely that the percentage of GDP is somewhat higher.

[11] The objective has been set to transfer 25 per cent of energy use to local, alternative sources by 2012.

Box I.1. Belarus trade relations

Belarus is pursuing a busy trade negotiation agenda at both the multilateral and bilateral levels. These negotiations should prove of key importance to further opening the economy and to moving forward other structural transformations.

At the multilateral level, a fundamental process of negotiation of accession to the WTO has been going on since 1995. Since June 1997, seven formal sessions of the WTO working party on Belarus' accession were held, the latest of which took place on 24 May 2005. Two key aspects of WTO accession negotiations are at play. First, Belarus' market access negotiations for goods are of strategic importance to its trade with the EU and the United States. Different sensitivities are noticeable. Historically, Belarus has been subject to one of the tightest bilateral textile trade regimes from EU import policies. In October 2008, however, import conditions on textile products became more favourable to Belarus when the EU cancelled its textile quotas on 13 out of 31 tariff lines. On the other hand, just a year earlier, in June 2007, the EU withdrew preferences for Belarus under the generalized system of preferences (GSP) on the grounds of inconsistencies in minimum labour standards regulations. The second challenging issue facing Belarus in its WTO accession negotiations is whether it will be considered a market economy. This would be particularly important concerning the use of anti-dumping and countervailing measures on certain Belarusian pricing and incentive practices. In addition, WTO negotiations involve many other complex issues ranging from agriculture to trade in services.

Another process at the multilateral level is the creation of the Eurasian Economic Community (EurAsEC) in October 2000. Belarus, along with the other five members (Kazakhstan, Kyrgyzstan, the Russian Federation, Tajikistan and Uzbekistan) decided to create a common market and adopt a unified system of customs tariffs and non-tariff measures. The key priority of this union is the harmonization of economic policies including those on energy, transport and trade. While some progress has been made, including the signature in December 2008 of a Treaty on the Promotion and Mutual Protection of Investments among member states, the free movement of goods, services, capital and people has not yet been achieved. The most advanced integration effort towards a full customs union so far is that between Belarus, Kazakhstan and the Russian Federation, which remains open to other EurAsEc members.

With respect to bilateral arrangements, as of 2008, Belarus had concluded 60 agreements on trade and economic cooperation. Among these agreements, 40 countries grant most favoured nation treatment to imports from Belarus. Additionally, Belarus is currently negotiating another 35 agreements. The most recent negotiations on trade cooperation began in 2007 with China, Nicaragua, Oman, Serbia, the Syrian Arab Republic and Viet Nam.

Source: UNCTAD.

Figure I.2. Key policies affecting private sector development in Belarus, 1991–2008

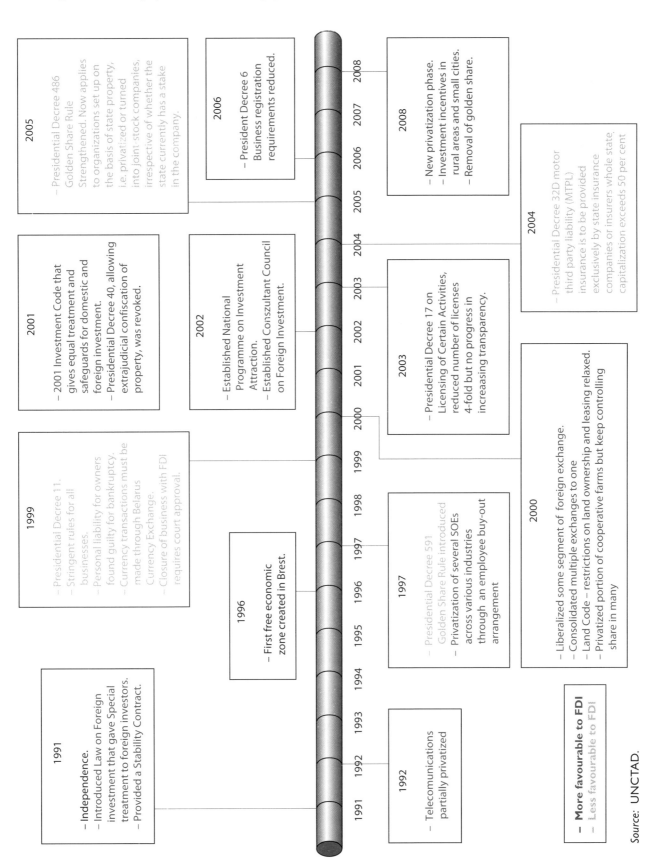

B. FDI trends and policies

1. Total FDI inflows

Since independence and until very recently, policies affecting FDI, and more generally private sector development in Belarus, have followed a volatile pattern. Figure I.2 shows how dirigisme and economic liberalization have frequently intertwined. For instance, in 1994, Belarus launched its first attempt at privatizing some public assets and companies (box I.2). In 1997, however, the government introduced the "Golden Share Rule", which allowed public interference in the management of partially privatized companies. In 2005, the provision was revised so as to apply irrespective of whether the state maintained or not a stake in the privatized asset. The Golden Share Rule was however not exercised extensively. According to official information, it was exercised in 14 joint-stock companies out of 1,600 (EBRD, 2006). It nevertheless generated perplexity in the investor community about undue public interference in the economy. It was eventually removed in 2008 as part of the initiatives to improve the overall investment climate.

The ambiguous policy stance vis-à-vis private sector development and the frequent policy reversals have also raised predictability issues on the investment climate in Belarus, which critically impacted private investment, both domestic and foreign. As a result, total FDI inflows to Belarus remained fairly low with the exception of 2007 (figure I.3), both in absolute terms and relative to other CIS and similar transition economies (table I.1).

Figure I.3.   FDI inflows to Belarus, 1992–2007
(Millions of dollars)

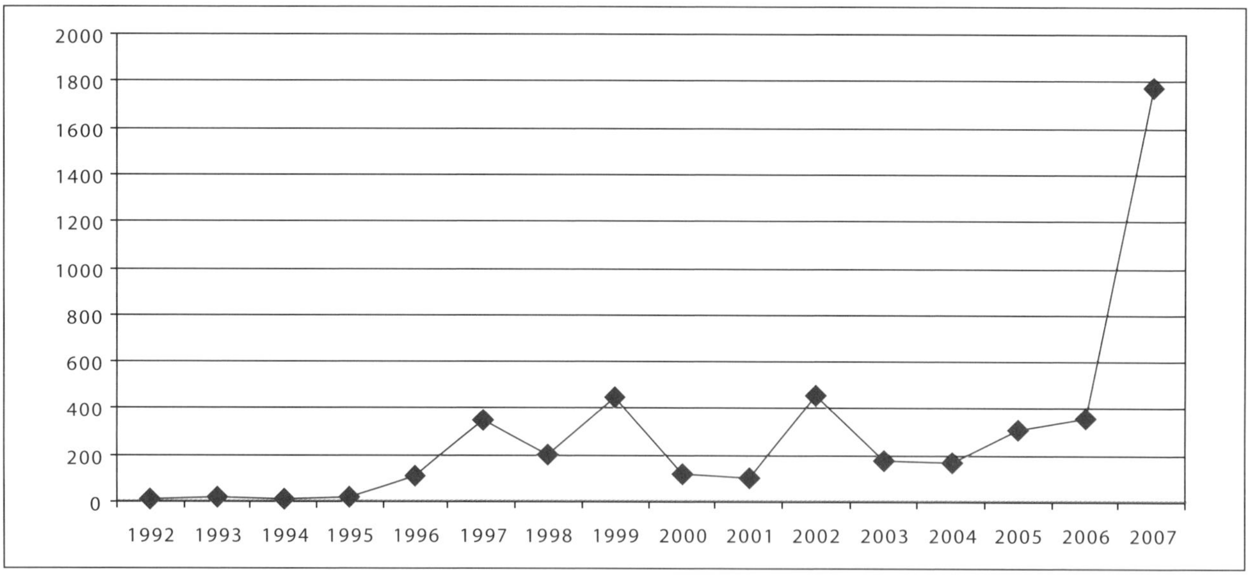

Source: 1992–1996 World Investment Report; 1997–2007 Belarus Central Bank.

The 2007 surge in FDI can be attributed largely to one-off investments, such as Russian State-owned Gazprom's first payment of $625 million toward its 50 per cent share of Beltransgaz and SB Telecom's $500 million purchase of state-owned shares of mobile telecom company MDC (a joint venture formed in 1999 between SB Telecom, Beltelecom and the closed joint-stock company Beltechexport, box I.4). It is also possible that FDI inflows have reacted positively to initial reforms carried out over between 2007 and 2009. This is supported by the perception of stakeholders in the private sector, including foreign investors, which concurs that policy has been consistently moving in the direction of reducing restrictions and administrative pressure on business.[12] However, scepticism remains on the receptiveness, at the operational level of the government, to effectively implement the required cultural and administrative changes in the absence of an explicit and widely discussed private sector development strategy.

---

[12]   UNCTAD mission to Belarus, May 2008.

Among the reforms introduced since the beginning of 2008 are the streamlining of the business registration process, the removal of the controversial Golden Share Rule and the enactment of more than 60 decrees and edicts affecting various aspects of doing business. Most reforms emanate directly from the President's legislative activity. They include further streamlining of registration and licensing requirements and the introduction of new incentive schemes for investment in priority areas such as rural or small towns. A new round of privatization was also launched in July 2008, and contrary to the former privatization programme, it openly targets foreign investors in different sectors (box.I.2). The second chapter of this report analyses these policy initiatives in greater detail.

Box I.2. The privatization process in Belarus – past and present

Belarus officially began privatization as early as 1991. Most transactions took place between 1994 and 1996. The main targets of the programme were companies in retail trade and public catering (restaurants or food stands), agri-business, light industry, construction and unprofitable enterprises in all fields of the economy, except those where privatization was prohibited. Between 1991 and 1996, the process involved a total of 526 enterprises. The majority of them were reformed into joint-stock companies using the voucher system, whereby each citizen received a voucher that could be exchanged for shares in the privatized SOEs, while auctions or biddings were utilized for enterprises in communal property, small trade business or consumer services. In the case of joint-stock companies, 2,002 enterprises were reformed using this method. However in one third of the reformed companies, the government retained 69 per cent ownership, considerably curtailing the extent of privatization.

Privatization in Belarus

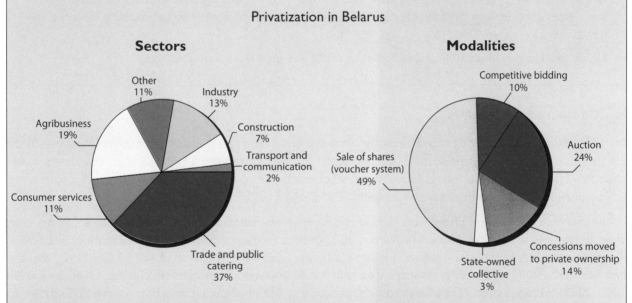

Source: Belarus State Property Fund (2008), supplemented by www.belarus.by.

Between 1996 and 2007, the scope and pace of privatization slowed down significantly due notably to a lack of investor interest. Furthermore, until 2002, there was no real foreign participation in the process. This was indeed limited to the sale of an agriculture enterprise for approximately $210 million. However over the last six years, foreign participation has increased, though concentrated on few assets. Examples include the $500 million sale of remaining state-owned shares of MDC to SB Telecom, the recent $2.5 billion Beltransgaz agreement with the Russian Federation and the $500 million sale of BeST to Turkcell.

(continues on next page)

(continued)

There are a number of factors behind the lack of investors' interest in the past privatization effort. In the first place, many of the assets for sale consisted of loss-making SOEs, hardly attractive for either domestic or foreign investors. Second, the government introduced a moratorium on the sale and purchase of vouchers at the beginning of the privatization initiative that negatively affected the vouchers' redemption rates. As a result, the government extended the "term of use" on vouchers five times. By 2003, nine years after the programme started, as much as 47 per cent of vouchers had not been redeemed for shares, corresponding to a $400 million government liability or 12 per cent of the annual budget. This is an important figure because by law unused vouchers may be redeemed for cash at face value at the end of the privatization programme (now vouchers can be redeemed only after 30 June 2010). Ultimately, cash at the end of the privatization initiative became more attractive than non-tradable shares of the worst performing SOEs. Lastly, international agencies assessing the process concluded that the valuation methodology lacked transparency and impartiality. In this regard, the primary criticism was that the State Property Fund that was overseeing the valuation of assets created a conflict of interest.

In 2008, the government launched a new and enlarged privatization programme and committed to privatize more attractive assets in a transparent and open manner. It also decided to phase out the moratorium on the sale of vouchers and explicitly target FDI. Decree 1021 of 2008 of the Council of Ministers confirmed that 519 enterprises were to be privatized between 2008 and 2010. The list includes companies from light manufacturing, wood industry, construction, machine building and metal plants. For the first time, the privatization extends to assets formerly considered as strategic, such as the Minsk Automobile Plant. Valuation methodology, however, remains unchanged, although the State Property Fund guarantees that certified specialists will conduct the valuation using international standards.

Sources: State Property Fund (2008), UNCTAD interviews, IMF (2004 and 2005) and www.belarus.by.

2. Comparative FDI flows

The Belarusian authorities have recently set ambitious FDI targets, including raising FDI inflows from 2.6 per cent of total investment to 15–20 per cent. This would require a significant improvement in the country's FDI attraction performance, which has been sub-par compared to other Eastern European and CIS countries, at least until the one-off surge in FDI inflows in 2007.

In terms of absolute FDI inflows, out of the sample of comparator countries, Belarus has been an underperformer since 1991 (table I.1). Across all countries in the sample, with the exception of Belarus, Kyrgyzstan and Uzbekistan, average FDI inflows increased between the second half of the 1990s and the first half of the 2000s, reflecting, in most cases, reforms to improve the investment climate. Over the period 2001–2005, average annual FDI inflows to Belarus stood at $197 million, i.e. one third of the FDI inflows to Lithuania ($632 million) and one half of the FDI inflows to Latvia ($408 million). Belarus' FDI stock reflects a similar situation. Belarus' FDI attraction performance significantly improved in 2007 as a result of the large FDI inflows.

In relative terms, Belarus is generally lagging, only placing ahead of Uzbekistan and much smaller economies such as Kyrgyzstan and Tajikistan. The share of FDI in the economy, an average of 2.5 per cent of GDP (over the period 2006–2007), is fairly low, particularly in comparison to the CIS average of 4.1 per cent and the Eastern Europe and Central Asia average of 5.2 per cent. As a share of gross fixed capital formation, FDI to Belarus has also been historically lower than in the other countries in the comparison. And it declined from 7.4 per cent in the period 1996–2000 to 4.4 per cent in the period 2001–2005. Due to the large inflow in 2007, it stood at 8 per cent for the period 2006–2007.

Table I.I. Comparative performance of Belarus with selected countries, 1991–2007
(Dollars and percentage)

Country	ABSOLUTE PERFORMANCE Average FDI inflows per year — Millions of dollars				ABSOLUTE FDI Stock Millions of dollars	RELATIVE PERFORMANCE Average FDI inflows per year — Per capita (Dollars)				Per $1000 GDP				As per cent of gross fixed capital formation				FDI Stock Per capita (Dollars)	FDI Stock Per $1000 GDP
	1991–1995	1996–2000	2001–2005	2006–2007	2007	1991–1995	1996–2000	2001–2005	2006–2007	1991–1995	1996–2000	2001–2005	2006–2007	1991–1995	1996–2000	2001–2005	2006–2007	2007	2007
Belarus*	**12.5**	**244.4**	**196.7**	**1 063.1**	**4 499.5**	**1.2**	**24.1**	**20**	**110.1**	**0.8**	**18.7**	**10.3**	**24.6**	**0.3**	**7.4**	**4.4**	**8**	**466**	**10**
Azerbaijan*	59	595	2'010.8	-2'709	6'597.6	7.6	74.6	241.4	-317.6	18.9	149.5	285.6	-96.2	11.5	45.1	53.8	-45.7	773	22.4
Georgia	4.7	155.2	310	1'359.4	5'259	0.9	32.1	68.3	308.2	1.8	46.5	66.4	149	1.3	20.8	24.7	55.6	1'196	51.1
Kyrgyzstan*	48.1	56.2	54.6	195	818.5	10.5	11.8	10.5	36.4	33.7	34.6	25.3	60	20.5	24.5	17.3	35.7	152	21.8
Latvia	117.7	403.9	407.9	1'918.4	10'493	46.4	167.3	175.7	838.2	23.8	60.8	32.2	81.7	17	30.9	12.1	25.1	4'595	38.6
Lithuania	36.3	459.6	632.4	1'887.2	14'679	9.9	129.7	183.3	553.4	5.5	42.9	34.5	56.1	2.5	19.4	16.3	22	4'313	38.3
Republic of Moldova*	27.5	68.7	121.9	350.6	1'812.8	6.3	16	28.8	83.7	14.3	46.1	56.4	87.7	8.8	285.9	30.4	33.2	433	41.2
Poland	1'657.2	6'476.8	7'577.6	18'389	142'110	43	167.6	196.5	477.8	14.7	38.9	31.6	49	8.8	16.9	16.9	23.6	3'694	33.8
Russian Federation*	1'281.8	3'245.8	8'499.5	42'431.2	324'065.4	8.6	22	59	298.5	3	11.2	16.1	36.8	1.4	6.8	8.8	18.6	2'284	25.1
Slovenia	111.1	193.1	747.8	1'035.7	10'349.8	56.9	98.2	380.2	527	8.3	9.5	28.7	24	3.9	4	11.9	8.6	5'268	22.5
Tajikistan*	10	19.2	77.1	369.6	1'045.9	1.8	3.2	12	55.7	6.6	18.6	40.4	114.2	4	16.8	47.4	105.7	156	28.2
Ukraine*	206.5	595.6	2'486.4	7747.5	38'059	4	11.9	53	169.6	3.5	15.3	36.5	61	1.4	7.7	17.1	23.3	836	27
Uzbekistan*	26.5	118.5	98.7	228.3	1'648.4	1.2	4.9	3.8	8.4	2	7.8	8.9	11.9	0.8	2.6	3.9	5.5	60	7.4
Commonwealth of Independent States (CIS)	**2'012**	**6'581**	**17'031**	**60'601**	**433'563**	**8.3**	**23.3**	**61.1**	**219.1**	**4.5**	**16.6**	**25.5**	**40.6**	**2.3**	**9.1**	**13**	**18.8**	**1'569**	**26**
Eastern Europe and Central Asia	**8'372**	**24'267**	**46'960**	**132'849**	**1'013'033**	**20.6**	**59.8**	**116.4**	**330.5**	**9.8**	**30.7**	**36.1**	**52**	**4.4**	**14.4**	**17.4**	**23.4**	**2'521**	**35.3**
Developing economies	**77'906**	**202'735**	**233'122**	**456'368**	**4'246'738**	**17.9**	**42.4**	**45.8**	**86.5**	**15.6**	**31.2**	**28.2**	**34.2**	**6.4**	**13**	**11.5**	**12.5**	**792**	**29.8**

Source: UNCTAD.
Note: *CIS country.

3. Private investment and FDI in GDP

The structure of the Belarusian economy remained fairly stable between 1995 and 2006 (figure 1.4). Furthermore, heavy regulation of the business environment, price controls[13] and the dominance of the state in most sectors of the economy resulted in an underdeveloped private sector. As a result, the contribution of private enterprises to GDP stands at a low 25 per cent while SMEs contribute 8.1 per cent to GDP. Chapter III of this report analyses the SME sector in more detail.

Figure 1.4.   GDP by sector in Belarus, 1995 and 2006
(Percentage)

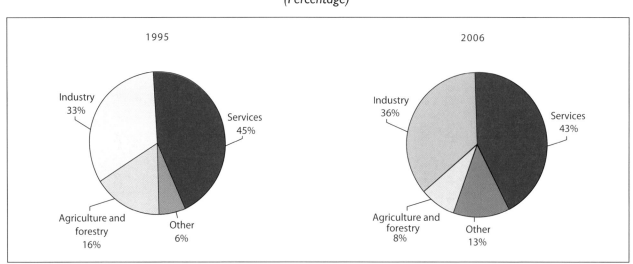

Source: Statistical Yearbook of the Republic of Belarus 2007.
*Other: FISIM (financial intermediation services indirectly measured), taxes, subsidies.

The data on the distribution of FDI inflows by sector between 2002 and 2007 (figure 1.5) indicate that the large majority are concentrated in the services sector (79 per cent), followed by industry (20 per cent). FDI in agriculture is negligible (1 per cent of the total). The sections below provide more details on each sector.

Figure 1.5.   Belarus: FDI inflows by sector, 2002–2007
(Percentage)

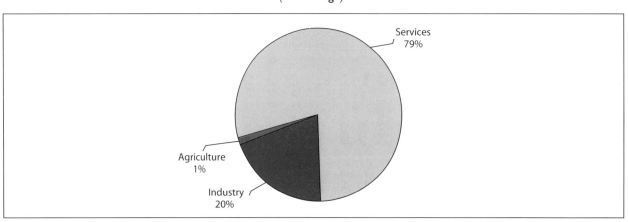

Source: Ministry of Economy of Belarus.

---

[13] According to the International Finance Corporation (IFC) survey of the Belarusian SME sector (2006), 61 per cent of respondents said that prices of certain goods and services were regulated by the state. Of those, 71 per cent indicated that all of their goods and services were subject to price regulation.

Industry

In industry, nearly two thirds of the enterprises are in private hands, including 2.5 per cent of foreign companies (table I.2). In terms of output and employment, however, fully private firms are fairly small, representing only about 13 per cent and 22 per cent of the total. Joint ventures between SOEs and local private enterprises account for the largest share of total output in industry, but the largest employers remain the SOEs, which account for 40 per cent of total industry employment.

Table I.2. The industrial sector in Belarus by type of ownership

(Percentage)

	Enterprises	Output	Employment
State	25.6	34.4	40.2
Partially private			
State and private joint ventures (no foreign investment)	10.6	45.6	31.6
State and private joint ventures (with foreign investment)	4.1	6.8	6.6
Fully private			
Local private companies	57.2	10.8	19.2
Foreign private companies	2.5	2.4	2.4

Source: Statistical Yearbook of the Republic of Belarus 2007.

Table I.3 presents the distribution of industrial output by main activity and the share of FDI in each activity. Together, oil and gas refinement and related activities account for one third of all industrial output. Other traditional industrial activities include machine building, such as tractors and heavy load trucks (24 per cent of industrial output), food processing and fertilizers. FDI in industry is low (never exceeding more than 6 per cent of output in any activity), but quite diversified across activities including timber and wood products, agro-processing (mainly beverages and fish processing), chemicals, machine building and light industry.

Table I.3. 2006 total industrial output by activity and share of FDI per activity

(Percentage)

	Contribution to industrial output	FDI share in activity
Electric power	5.9	0
Fuel industry	21.8	0.7
Chemical and petrochemical industry	11.2	2
Ferrous metallurgy	3.6	0.7
Machine building and metal working	23.8	2.1
Timber, woodworking and pulp and paper	4.4	6
Construction materials	4.3	0.2
Light industry	4.4	2.2
Food/agro-processing	18.4	3.4

Source: Statistical Yearbook of the Republic of Belarus 2007, section 14.

Although no precise analysis is possible on the basis of available data, it is estimated that a large share of FDI in industry is located in the country's six free economic zones (FEZs) (box I.3).

Box I.3. Belarus' free economic zones

In 1996, Belarus created its first FEZ in Brest with the objective of creating favourable conditions for investment and for the development of regions. The goal was also to implement progressive, environmentally friendly technology and promote international integration and cooperation. Today, the state owns and operates FEZs in each of the six regions of the country. The FEZs in Minsk and Brest report the largest share of the 260 FEZ investors (i.e. investors within the zones) with 67 and 76 respectively. The majority of FEZ investors are engaged in manufacturing. For example, in the Minsk FEZ, for which detailed statistics are available, 60 per cent of investors are engaged in mechanical engineering and metal working.

Just over half of total investment flowing into the zones is FDI. In 2007, FDI to the FEZs equalled $64.3 million, which represents only 4 per cent of total FDI inflows to the country for that year. This may appear low compared to the average share of country-wide FDI attracted to FEZs in Central and Eastern Europe and Central Asia, which stands at over 35 per cent, but one has to take into account the exceptional surge in non-FEZ FDI in that year. In terms of export performance, however, the contribution of the FEZs in Belarus to total exports from the country (4.1 per cent) is close to the average for FEZs in Central and Eastern Europe and Central Asia (6.1 per cent). Available data on the Minsk FEZ indicates that the countries of origin of FDI to the FEZs are fairly diversified, although the greatest share of resident companies is from the United Kingdom.

2007 Minsk FEZ: FDI by industrial sector and originating country

Sector

- Pulp, paper and woodworking 7%
- Other 1%
- Packing 7%
- Communication devices and radio electronics 9%
- Chemical and petrochemical 8%
- Building materials 9%
- Mechanical engineering, metal working 59%

Country of origin

- United States 8%
- Sweden 3%
- Cyprus 10%
- Germany 7%
- Russian Federation 13%
- Others 6%
- Netherlands 5%
- Latvia 4%
- Kazakhstan 2%
- United Kingdom 42%

Among the likely reasons for the low performance of the FEZs in FDI attraction is the lengthy permit issuance process (reportedly requiring over a year) and stringent entry requirements. Investment projects are admitted to the FEZs based on a case-by-case assessment of how well they conform to the social and economic policy of the state. Other criteria include that 70 per cent or more of production is destined for export unless the product is on the list of import substitution goods and that more than 90 per cent of imported production equipment is not more than five years old.

In 2008, Edict 42 introduced an additional minimum investment requirement of €1 million. It also introduced benefits such as exemption from the foreign exchange tax and from a compulsory deduction for the Ministry of Architecture and Construction's Innovation fund. Other benefits for residents that were maintained included tax exemptions such as a five-year exemption from profit tax and thereafter a cap of profit tax at half the normal rate, exemption from real estate tax, some customs preferences such as no import duties, and no export duties on goods exported to the Russian Federation or outside Belarus or domestically if the product is on the import substitution list (see chapter II for details).

Sources: UNCTAD interviews, Bearing Point (2004), Ministry of Foreign Affairs and Ministry of Economy (2008).

Agriculture

Agriculture is a shrinking sector that currently represents about 8 per cent of GDP (figure I.4). Historically, the sector has been managed through a system of collectives[14] and strict leasing policies.[15] With the relaxation of the policy on land leases and ownership in the early 2000s,[16] household plots and small private farms have started gaining importance. These plots and private farms now produce nearly half of all agricultural output while accounting for only 20 per cent of land area.[17] Notwithstanding the increase in private farming, the sector remains firmly in the hands of the state with three quarters of all agri-business run by state-controlled enterprises including inputs and farm services.[18] The profitability performance of the cooperatives and the agro-businesses has unfortunately been sub-par, requiring government subsidies to sustain the system. Foreign investment in the sector is also very limited, amounting to only I per cent of total FDI inflows between 2002 and 2007.

Services

The services sector contributed 43 per cent to GDP in 2006, a figure largely unchanged since 1995. Within services, trade and catering (10.3 per cent) and transport (6.7 per cent) accounted for the highest share of total GDP in 2006, a consistent trend since 1995. Construction services have become increasingly important. In 2006, they accounted for 7.9 per cent of GDP, a reflection of the construction boom currently underway.

The service sector is the sector where FDI is most visible, particularly in banking and telecommunications. At the end of 2006, there were 30 banks in Belarus, most of which are either joint-stock or limited liability companies; 26 banks had foreign capital, including 10 that were wholly foreign-owned. The foreign share of the bank sector's assets stood at 14.7 per cent and foreign aggregate capital (FDI and portfolio) in the sector totalled 7.8 per cent in 2006 (Central Bank of Belarus, 2006). Among the foreign banks, with the exception of Raiffeisen (Austria), mainly minor banks have been attracted to the Belarusian market from a variety of countries including Poland (Alpha Bank), Switzerland (BelSwissBank) and Lithuania (Techno Bank).

The mobile telecommunications sector has developed largely through FDI (see the section on the impact of FDI below and box I.4). In 1999, a Cypriot firm, SB Telecom, entered the market through a joint venture with state-owed telecom enterprises and started the first mobile company, Mobile Digital Communications (MDC). It marketed mobile calling services through Velcom and invested $500 million. A Russian company, Mobile TeleSystems (MTS), entered the market in 2002 through a joint venture with Beltelecom and now holds 49 per cent of the shares. It also invested $700 million in network expansion. In 2007, Austria Telkom purchased a 70 per cent stake in SB Telecom for nearly $1 billion, becoming the new owner of MDC, reflecting the continued attractiveness of the Belarus mobile market. The latest purchase of 80 per cent in state-owned BeST by Turkcell for a reported $500 million is a further indication of the sector's attractiveness to foreign investors.

Retail and construction are two other services sectors that received foreign investment, although to a lesser extent. FDI in the retail sector has come to Belarus in the form of hypermarkets such as the Russian company Vester, and FINOX, a joint Belarus–United States venture. The recent growth in construction has also benefited from foreign investment. In 2006, a Russian firm, Moscow Investment Construction Company, began a $161 million project to build residential housing in Minsk. Two other large projects are currently

---

[14] Agricultural production based on common ownership of resources and on pooling of labour and income and managed through state enterprises or under the direct supervision of the state.

[15] Until the early 2000s, private property rights (up to one hectare) did not provide for property registration nor market transactions.

[16] These came about starting with the "Programme for the improvement of the agro-industrial sector 2001–2005" and continued with the "Programme for the revival and development of the rural areas 2005–2010".

[17] These figures are for 2003. A 2000 study by the World Bank reported that household plots accounted for 14 of 15 private farms (World Bank, 2005).

[18] As of 2003: collective (2 per cent), state farm (1 per cent), cooperative (55 per cent), joint-stock (15 per cent). Ibid.

being carried out by an Iranian firm, Keyson Prilesie. The first project to build a logistics centre in the Minsk FEZ began in 2005 with an investment of $150 million. The second project that began in 2008 was for the construction of a hotel and convention complex in the city of Minsk with an investment of $236 million. The largest project underway, however, was begun late 2007 by Latvian firm, UAB Ûkio Banko Investicinë Grupë (ÛBIG), which is investing $350 million to build the new Minsk Leisure Centre, an enlargement and modernization of the Minsk Traktor Stadium (ÛBIG , 2007).

4. FDI by country of origin

It was not possible to obtain official data on the distribution of FDI by country of origin. Nevertheless, observation and interviews with stakeholders in the public and private sectors suggest that the Russian Federation is the most important source of FDI to Belarus, followed by Western European countries (mainly Austria, Germany and Italy). Neighbouring countries, such as Latvia and Poland, have also started investing in Belarus in the recent past.

C. Impact of FDI

The impact of FDI on a country's economic and social development is generally measured in terms of its positive contribution to output, employment, export diversification, technology and skills transfer, and supplier linkages, as well as fiscal revenues and infrastructure development. However, FDI can also have negative effects on the development of domestic enterprises and the performance of an economy, particularly when it enters highly protected markets.

Belarus has a relatively recent history of FDI attraction and the low volume of FDI inflows so far implies that the impact on its economy is limited. Nevertheless, in those sectors with significant FDI presence, such as telecommunications and banking, it is possible to observe effects such as a considerable improvement in services delivery and a reduction in costs. Transnational corporations (TNCs) are large contributors to the country's trade flows, although their imports largely outweigh their exports. The following section presents an impact assessment that is drawn from available data and anecdotal or ancillary information.

1. Employment and output

As shown in figure I.6, although employment by TNCs and joint ventures with foreign participation represents only a small percentage of total employment, it has been increasing steadily since the early 1990s. In 2006, employment by foreign investors and joint ventures between the state and foreign companies totalled 180,000 employees or 4.1 per cent of total employment. A comparison with the contribution of TNCs and joint ventures with foreign participation to total output of goods and services, which stands at 17 per cent (Ministry of Statistics and Analysis (MSA), 2007), suggests higher levels of productivity in foreign-invested enterprises. This could be explained by a number of factors, including different capital intensity of production, more efficient production techniques or higher labour productivity.

Figure I.6 also shows a significant reduction in employment by SOEs in favour of employment by the local private sector in the years immediately following independence (1991–1995). Since 2000, however, the increase in the share of private sector employment is less marked, and largely explained by an increase in employment by foreign investors or state-foreign joint ventures.

Figure I.6. Employment in Belarus by ownership type, 1990–2006

(Percentage)

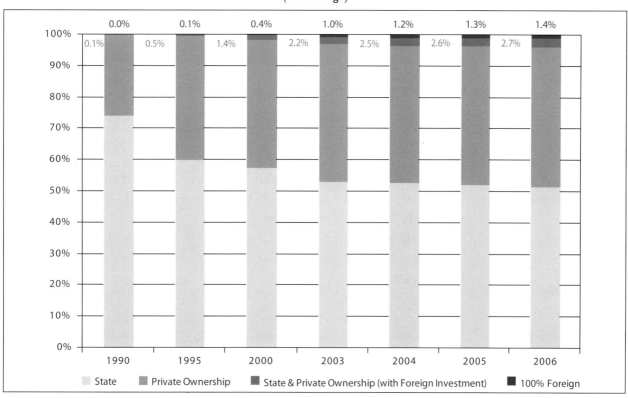

Source: Statistical Yearbook of the Republic of Belarus 2007.

2. Linkages

Interviews with both domestic and foreign investors in Belarus, carried out by UNCTAD in the context of this review, indicate that the establishment of supplier linkages is particularly problematic. SMEs play a limited role in the economy and are concentrated in the retail sector. They are particularly affected by a heavy regulatory burden and price controls. They also face difficulties in becoming suppliers not only to large TNCs but also to the local industry. Apart from issues of quality, cost and standards of production, there is a perception that SMEs are ill-equipped to respond to the needs of large firms that are traditionally vertically integrated. The status of the SME sector in Belarus as well as the role of FDI in supporting its development is the focus of chapter III of this report. The chapter also contains a more detailed analysis of the linkages problem.

3. Technology transfer

Technology transfer encompasses both the physical transfer of machinery and technology as well as the intangible transfer of knowledge and skills. Assessing whether FDI has had a positive impact in this area requires a comparative analysis of factors such as the introduction of new quality control processes, just-in-time inventory strategies, the level of automation of production and its technology intensity. No such analysis was carried out for the purpose of this report and the available literature on the subject is scarce. The employment figures mentioned above suggest that foreign investors do make use of more innovative production processes. However, the very limited presence of supplier linkages and the low levels of FDI, especially in industry and agriculture, suggest that a significant technological impact is unlikely.

Recent policy initiatives in the area of investment, such as the TechnoPark incentive scheme, which is aimed at attracting investors to high value added and technology-intensive sectors (see chapter II), the new round of privatization (box I.2) and the focus on attracting private investment to agriculture, all indicate a willingness to attract private capital to sectors where new technology and modernization is needed.

4. Trade

Belarus' foreign trade is oriented primarily towards the Russian Federation, with whom a free trade area has been in force since 1995. Table I.4 shows that the main countries of origin of Belarusian imports have remained the same since year 2000.

Table I.4.   Belarus: top five export and import partners

2000			2007		
Country of import	Total (thousands of dollars)	%	**Country of import**	Total (thousands of dollars)	%
Russian Federation	5'549.7	64	Russian Federation	17'204.9	60
Germany	587.6	7	Germany	2'171.4	8
Ukraine	340.6	4	Ukraine	1'534.3	5
Poland	215.8	3	Poland	819.1	3
Italy	162.6	2	China	815.8	3
Country of export	Total (thousands of dollars)	%	**Country of export**	Total (thousands of dollars)	%
Russian Federation	3'715.7	51	Russian Federation	8'878.6	37
Ukraine	559.7	8	Netherlands	4'277.3	18
Latvia	467.3	6	United Kingdom	1'528.9	6
Lithuania	348.8	5	Ukraine	1'469.8	6
Poland	276.8	4	Poland	1'226.2	5

Source: UNCTAD, COMTRADE Database.

The largest exporter to Belarus is the Russian Federation, which remains the only source of oil and natural gas and also a large exporter of raw materials for manufacturing activities such as metals and chemicals. In terms of exports, however, the Russian Federation's prominence is diminishing (from 51 per cent of total exports in 2000 to 37 per cent in 2007) in favour of the EU, particularly the Netherlands (destination of 18 per cent of exports in 2007) and the United Kingdom (6 per cent of exports in 2007). The composition of Belarusian exports, which has not changed significantly over time, is represented by oil and oil products (31 per cent of total exports), machinery and equipment (20 per cent of total exports) and fertilizers (6.3 per cent of total exports).

The contribution of foreign investors to total trade in Belarus is increasingly significant, particularly in light of the limited volume of FDI in the economy. In 2006, companies with foreign participation, including fully foreign-owned companies, accounted for 33 per cent of total imports (up from 8 per cent in 2000) and 24 per cent of exports (up from 9 per cent in 2000) (table I.5).

In the absence of a breakdown of exports by TNCs and by product, it is not possible to assess the extent of the contribution of FDI to the country's recent diversification in export destinations. It is nevertheless possible to observe that foreign-invested enterprises appear to have a negative impact on Belarus' trade balance, and more so than domestic firms, pointing to the necessity of stimulating local supplier linkages.

Table I.5.   Belarusian imports and exports in 2000 and 2006

(Millions of dollars and percentage)

	2000		2006	
	Total (millions of dollars)	%	Total (millions of dollars)	%
Total imports	8'646	100	22'351	100
Domestic firms	7'950	92	14'970	67
Firms with foreign participation	696	8	7'381	33
Joint ventures	506	5.9	2'810	12.6
100% foreign	190	2.2	4'571	20.5
Total exports	7'326	100	19'734	100
Domestic firms	6'635	90.6	14'945	75.7
Firms with foreign participation	691	9.4	4'789	24.3
Joint ventures	445	6.1	2'136	10.8
100% foreign	246	3.4	2'653	13.4

Source: Belarus Statistical Yearbook 2007.

5.   Backbone services

The role of FDI in the development of backbone services has been limited to mobile telecommunications, as other infrastructure services such as fixed telecommunications or power generation have not yet been opened to FDI. However, proposals to allow FDI in fixed telecommunications are currently being considered (as required for WTO accession), and the government is actively seeking foreign investors in waste management, alternative energy production and road construction. In this respect, the authorities should consider introducing a legal framework for the advancement of public-private partnerships (PPPs) as an approach to attract private investment, including FDI, to infrastructure projects.

The history of the mobile telecommunications sector is described in box I.4 and is a reflection of the instability that characterized the Belarusian investment climate until 2007. In terms of the impact of FDI, however, it is a success story. The first foreign investment in the sector took place in 1993, but it was only after 1999, when two more mobile operators were licensed, that competition in the sector picked up. The effects on the reduction of communications costs and expansion of the subscriber base were impressive, as figure I.7 and box I.4 reveal. Belarus now has the fourth largest subscriber base in the region and a three-minute peak call costs just $0.11, as compared to $2.83 in 1998.

Box I.4. Mobile telephony in Belarus

The history of mobile telecommunications in Belarus illustrates how past policies towards FDI have often been erratic. However, it is also a success story in terms of the impact that the entry of foreign investors has had on the availability and cost of mobile telecommunication services.

In 1993, Belarus allowed its first FDI in telecommunications. A decade later, three foreign companies were operating in the country through joint ventures with the state:

1993: BelCel formed through a joint venture between the United Kingdom's Cable & Wireless (50 per cent; the company was later acquired by Dutch company CIB B.V.), state-owned fixed line monopoly Beltelecom (33 per cent) and Uzbek Trastbank (17 per cent).

1999: MDC formed through a joint venture comprising Cypriot SB Telecom (69.9 per cent), Beltelecom (0.1 per cent) and closed joint-stock company Beltechexport (a defense industry firm, 30 per cent).

2002: Russian firm MTS (49 per cent) and Beltelecom (51 per cent) formed a joint venture to introduce MTS into the Belarus market.

BelCel built the first mobile network in the 1990s but, by 1999, Belarus still had one of the lowest subscriber bases in the region (on average, mobile subscriptions were growing by 30 per cent per year in Belarus as opposed to 100 per cent in comparator countries[1]). After the entry of MDC and MTS, Belarus' subscription base soared and its growth began matching, and frequently surpassing, that of other countries in the region. The number of subscribers grew from just over 23'000 in 1998 to over 1.1 million in 2003. During this same period, access (mobile subscribers per 100 inhabitants) also increased, growing from less than 1 per cent to over 11 per cent. The newcomers stimulated infrastructural development and competition effects causing the price of calls (based on a three-minute peak rate call) to drop drastically, from nearly $3 in 1998 to $0.11 in 2005.

In 2004, the government reversed the opening trend that marked this period of growth and began increasing its presence in mobile telecommunications. Through a decree, the government redistributed all shares of MDC, with SB Telecom losing its controlling interest and the state increasing its ownership to 51 per cent. Another redistribution of shares by the state occurred in 2005 with BelCel. As a result, the government took over Trastbank's share, thereby increasing its participation to 50 per cent and equalling that of CIB B.V. As the state increased its presence in joint ventures, it also started its own mobile operator, BeST, with loans from the Chinese Government. BeST was intended to operate as a social institution focusing on providing universal access.

In August 2007, two years after the redistribution of shares and creation of BeST, the government changed again its approach to the sector and allowed SB Telecom to buy out the state's shares for $500 million. This made MDC the first 100 per cent foreign-owned mobile telecommunications company in Belarus. Two months later, Austria Telekom bought a controlling stake (70 per cent) in SB Telecom for approximately $1 billion and became the new majority shareholder of MDC. The latest sign that the government is committed to opening the sector to FDI is the recent sale of 80 per cent interest in BeST to the Turkish mobile company Turkcell. It is estimated that the deal was worth $500 million.

[1] Average annual mobile subscriber growth from 1996 through 1998 using 13 comparator countries from table I.1.

Sources: BelCel (2008), Austria Telekom (2007), Turkcell (2008), World Bank (2003) and German Economic Team (GET) (2007).

Figure I.7.   Mobile telecommunications in Belarus: subscribers and cost

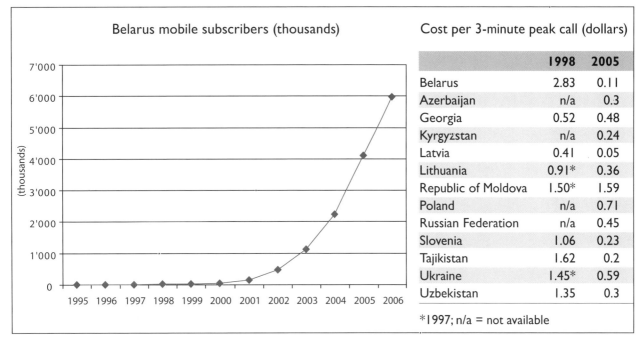

	1998	2005
Belarus	2.83	0.11
Azerbaijan	n/a	0.3
Georgia	0.52	0.48
Kyrgyzstan	n/a	0.24
Latvia	0.41	0.05
Lithuania	0.91*	0.36
Republic of Moldova	1.50*	1.59
Poland	n/a	0.71
Russian Federation	n/a	0.45
Slovenia	1.06	0.23
Tajikistan	1.62	0.2
Ukraine	1.45*	0.59
Uzbekistan	1.35	0.3

*1997; n/a = not available

Source: ITU World Telecommunication Indicators 2007.

D.   Assessment

Belarus has maintained a system of direct public management and operation of the economy aimed at improving living standards. In this context and until recently, private sector development and FDI attraction have not been prominent on the government's agenda and policies to promote both have long been cautious and often inconsistent.

Therefore, it is not surprising that Belarus has attracted low levels of FDI compared to most countries in the region. As a result, the impact of FDI on local economic development has been limited, with the exception of sectors where foreign investment has been actively encouraged, such as telecommunications and banking.

Since the end of 2007, the government has initiated a new cycle of reforms meant to progressively increase the contribution of the private sector to economic development. These include a new focus on improving the business climate and attracting increased and more diversified inflows of FDI, a task made more difficult by the global economic crisis. In this context, the challenge for Belarus is to regain investor confidence by presenting to both domestic and foreign investors its objectives and policies, in a transparent and open manner. Furthermore, the government needs to enforce effective implementation of coherent reforms at all levels of the administration. At the same time, the government should focus on putting in place appropriate mechanisms to ensure that local investors, and SMEs in particular, can benefit from the increased economic activity that would result from higher levels of FDI inflows.

Belarus has a large untapped potential for FDI attraction given the quality of its infrastructure and human capital as well as its privileged location between Western Europe and the Russian Federation. However, unless the issues surrounding SOEs and competition, private sector development and credibility regarding business-friendly reforms are adequately addressed, it will be difficult to realize such potential. These challenges and possible mechanisms to address them are the focus of the following chapters.

CHAPTER II

THE INVESTMENT FRAMEWORK

The Government of Belarus has made FDI attraction a key policy objective. In his State of the Nation address to the Belarusian people and the National Assembly on 29 April 2008, the President set forth a new target, namely to advance Belarus to the list of the 30 countries with the best business climate.[19] It is against this ambitious objective that this chapter reviews the policy framework of Belarus and recommends improvements to the investment climate.

In line with its FDI objectives, the government has embarked upon a widespread reform effort since late 2007, as indicated in chapter I. This was geared partly towards liberalizing the economy and simplifying administrative requirements such as business registration and licensing, and partly towards lowering the cost of doing business in the country, including by reducing the number of taxes. As a result of these reforms, the regulatory and administrative burden on business has started decreasing, and this is acknowledged by both local and foreign investors.[20] In May 2008, the Advisory Council for Foreign Investments, the main dialogue platform between the Belarusian Government and foreign investors, indicated that "the speed and consistency of the recent reforms have raised legitimate hopes regarding the increase in Belarus' attractiveness as an investment location".[21]

However, many elements still inhibit private sector development. These include the excessive regulation of business activity, the inadequacy of the competition regime and the persistence of heavy wage and price controls. Moreover, most recent reforms have only partially been carried through and in practice a heavier regulatory approach to business is still in place at various levels of the administration. In this context, the spirit of the reforms needs to trickle down to the middle to lower ranks of the bureaucracy as well as to regional and local administrations, where key bottlenecks and a predominantly planned economy attitude persist.

A. Specific FDI measures

The first laws dealing with investment were passed in 1991. At that time, foreign and domestic investments were regulated in two separate laws. In 2001, the two laws were consolidated into a single investment code. Since then, the legal framework for foreign investment has undergone several modifications, almost on a yearly basis. As of December 2008, the investment regime is set by the Investment Code of 2001, as revised last in July 2008.[22] The Investment Code is a comprehensive set of rules that applies to investment activities and establishes the conditions, forms and guarantees that comprise part of the FDI regime.

1. Entry and establishment

Sectors open for FDI

According to the provisions of the Investment Code, all sectors of the national economy are open to FDI, with the exception of a few selected industries:[23] the defence and security industries of the Republic of Belarus unless special authorization is granted by the President of Belarus, and the manufacturing and distribution of narcotic, powerful and toxic substances as given in the list approved by the Ministry of Health of Belarus.

---

[19] Belarus ranked eighty-fifth among 181 economies in the World Bank Ease of Doing Business ranking for 2009.
[20] Belarus is also among the top ten reformers from the World Bank's Doing Business Report of 2009, with respect to the reforms carried out during 2007–2008.
[21] Dr. Klaus Baier's intervention at the plenary meeting of the Advisory Council for Foreign Investments, 30 May 2008, Minsk.
[22] The original Investment Code of the Republic of Belarus (Law 37-Ç of 2001) was amended by Law 313-3 of 2004, Law 325-3 of 2004, Law 159-3 of 2006 and finally by Law 372-3 of 2008.
[23] Article 5 in conjunction with article 78 of the Investment Code.

In addition, foreign investment in legal entities that occupy a monopoly position on the Belarusian market is permitted only with the approval of the Ministry of Economy.

Restrictions on FDI entry also exist in insurance and reinsurance and in banking and financial activities (see later in this section). The Investment Code sets forth special regimes for these activities as well as for the state registration of commercial organizations with foreign investment located in FEZs. [24]

In general, therefore, Belarus is open to foreign investment, while the few sectors where foreign investment is not allowed or restricted are straightforward and fairly standard.

Forms an investment can take

The Investment Code sets forth the forms a foreign investment can take in Belarus and regulates all the conditions for its entry and registration. In order for the provisions and regime of the code to apply, a foreign investment must take the form of a "commercial organization with foreign investment", which represents all investments above $20,000 and with the generation of profit as the main objective.

Investment in Belarus can take place either through a wholly-owned foreign affiliate, a joint venture or the granting of a concession. Other forms of investment may take place with a different minimum charter capital and specific procedures for their establishment as set forth by other pieces of legislation. However, such forms of organizations shall not be eligible for the benefits and facilities established by the Investment Code.

The establishment of a commercial organization with foreign investment may take place either through incorporation or through acquisition by a foreign investor of an interest (shares) in an existing legal entity. The commercial organization shall have the right to own subsidiaries and associated companies and to establish branches and representative offices in Belarus, which however will have not the status of legal entities.

Documentary procedures

All commercial organizations with foreign investment must undergo state registration. The documents necessary for their registration are listed in the code as are the various steps involved, the grounds for denial of registration and the appeal procedure. The conditions and procedures for registration and its refusal are such that the registration effectively resembles what would be considered a permitting procedure elsewhere (see below, in this section).

The time frame prescribed by the code for state registration is 15 days from the submission of the complete documentation. Presidential Decree 8 of 2007, however, adopted a new simplified procedure on state registration and liquidation of legal entities with the objective of bringing registration time down to five days. Nevertheless, as shown below, collecting the documentation necessary for registration can be problematic.

Failure by a commercial organization with foreign investment to comply with the procedure for the formation of the charter capital established by the code may serve as grounds for its liquidation by the courts.

Conditions and procedures for registration

Belarus has adopted a decentralized registration policy and the state registration of commercial organizations with foreign investments is generally carried out by the Minsk City Executive Committee

---

[24] As per Presidential Decree 11 of 1999, as amended by Presidential Decree 8 of 2007, which provides a list of the authorities competent to carry out the state registration.

and six Regional Executive Committees ("Oblispolkom" – one for each district of Belarus). In the case of banks and financial institutions, registration is carried out by the National Bank; the Ministry of Finance is responsible for registering insurance companies and the Ministry of Justice is responsible for Chambers of Commerce and Trade. Finally, the Administration of Free Economic Zones registers foreign investors in these zones (excluding banks and insurance companies).[25]

The legislation provides some room for Regional Executive Committees to define their competence, institutional structure and procedural steps of registration. Regional and City Executive Committees are entitled to delegate power to other executive authorities.[26]

The legal grounds for refusing a registration can be formal (inappropriate documents, application, person or authority), material (debt of the founder or prohibition to engage in commercial activities) or for other reasons prescribed by legislative acts.[27]

The right to appeal refusal in a court is also provided for. However, investors need to wait for a refusal before going to court. Importantly, the requirement for a guarantee letter to be issued by the local authorities, confirming the investor's right to locate its business at the place of allocation, is still part of the conditions set forth by the code and by some of the regional instructions, whereas it has been repealed in Presidential Decree 8. This kind of requirement inevitably requires the issue of property and title on land to be solved and adds a layer of procedure and unpredictability to the entry process.

Although contained in a single set of legislation and attached regulations applicable to foreign investment, and in spite of a clear list of documents required for state registration, the level of transparency and predictability of the registration process is not satisfactory. The decentralization to different regional committees has given rise to some contradiction and inconsistencies between the Investment Code, the relevant Presidential Decree and the instructions issued by the regional authorities in charge of state registration. Thus, registration requirements can differ from one competent authority to another depending on the location of the investment.

Land acquisition rights of foreign investors in Belarus

Land acquisition rights of foreign investors are regulated by the new Land Code and by Presidential Decree 667 of 2007.[28] While the Land Code establishes only common rules and forms of land acquisition for foreign investors, such as leasehold, right of temporary use of parcel based on concessions, succession by the foreign citizen of life ownership and private property, Presidential Decree 667 details the prescribed conditions and procedure.

A strict zoning rule imposing use of land according to its "targeted" (functional) purpose and to the conditions of the leasing contract, taken together with the fact that around 90 per cent of land is allocated to agricultural and forestry purposes, and that a proper market for land titles still needs to develop, make it necessary for many investors who need access to land to go through a rezoning procedure, mainly from agricultural land to land that can be used for industrial or commercial purposes.

This procedure, as discussed later in this chapter (see the section on land), is cumbersome and lacks predictability since the relevant regulation does not contain an exhaustive list of the criteria required to authorize such a transfer. Moreover, many are involved in the rezoning at different levels of the administration and the relevant regulations lack consistency with several executive acts such as the Decisions of the

---

[25] Article 14 of Presidential Decree 11 of 1999, as amended by Presidential Decree 8 of 2007.
[26] Ibid, article 14.
[27] Ibid, article 34.
[28] Land Code that came into force on 1 January 2009 and Presidential Decree 667 of 2007.

President or Council of Ministers, the State Programmes, the City Constructer Projects and the detailed social and economic development plans of the different regions (box II.1).

This lack of transparency and legal certainty makes the investment process lengthy and prone to arbitrary decisions. Furthermore, this does not facilitate investment by foreign entities into Belarus in a competitive international context.

Special entry conditions

State registration of banks. The conditions for foreign bank registration are transparent and leave no room for discretion. They combine a set of objective criteria, which set forth a list of required documents[29] and ownership threshold conditions.[30] Reciprocity is a condition for registration, allowing the authorities to refuse the registration of a bank with foreign investments on grounds that the country of origin does not allow Belarusian investments in banks on their territory.

Box II.1. Plans of Social and Economic Development in Belarus

The Belarusian economic and industrial policy is framed by its Plans of Social and Economic Development.[31] In some aspects, the plans are similar to sectoral strategies and policy papers used in most countries, as they call for policy initiatives to promote economy-wide as well as sectoral development. However, the plans in Belarus go further and can be detailed to the point of enumerating economic and social target indicators to be achieved in each of the field of the economy, including in purely commercially-oriented activities as well as listing specific projects calling for investment (domestic or foreign alike).

The plans are drafted for short- (one-year), medium- (five-year) and long-term (15-year) periods at the national and regional levels. They are frequently complemented by specific sectoral plans adopted at the regional level and consistent with the broader national and regional plans. Together they constitute a comprehensive hierarchy of targets and forecasts for the economic development of the country.

The plans vary in content and depth, but, as a rule, they are typically quite detailed in their planning and forecast of sectoral development. While medium-term and long-term plans must include quantitative and qualitative indicators of macroeconomic development, annual plans concentrate mostly on concrete manufacturing targets that include output, volume of investments, retail and wholesale turnover.

Source: Ministry of Commerce, other ministries and UNCTAD.

State registration of insurances. A special regime for the registration of foreign investors in insurance imposes additional conditions that are not covered by a consolidated legal act, but prescribed by acts of segmental character and purpose. Disqualification of foreign investors in several types of insurance activities in conjunction with the applied ownership limit (30 per cent) contributes to making the establishment of foreign insurances in Belarus problematic.[32] Furthermore, the sector is currently experiencing a reform process that, until completed, poses predictability risks to investors.

---

[29] Several documents form part of the registration package, including a statement of the decision to establish or participate in the establishment of a bank with foreign investments, documents confirming registration of a legal entity, the balance of the previous year confirmed by an audit assessment, a written approval by an authorized institute of the home country, a copy of the investor's passport and a declaration by the applicant's bank of solvency confirming the sources of funds being contributed to the charter capital and the fees for the acquisition of shares of a resident bank.

[30] Recently, this quota was increased from 25 to 50 per cent of the total charter fund of banks registered in Belarus (Resolution 129 of 2008 of the National Bank).

[31] Law of the Republic of Belarus 157-3 of 1998 on State Planning and Programmes of Social and Economic Development of the Republic of Belarus.

[32] Subsidiaries of foreign insurance companies and companies with foreign participation above 49 per cent cannot obtain a licence for activities such as life insurance and compulsory insurance. The volume (quota) of foreign investments into the insurance system of Belarus is established by Council of Ministers Resolution 1174 of 2006 and equals 30 per cent of the total insurance capital.

State registration in free economic zones. Although a new Law on Free Economic Zones was recently adopted,[33] the entry regime governing the establishment of investors in the FEZs is challenging. The law provides for a decentralized system whereby each zone has its own administrative rules. This has resulted in the discretionary power of every FEZ Administration to stipulate specific conditions for investors' establishment on its territory.

Despite the attempt to harmonize such conditions through the Resolution of the Council of Ministers on Some Questions of Functioning of Free Economic Zones on the Territory of the Republic of Belarus, which imposed a minimum common set of registration documents[34] and of entry criteria, including a minimum investment threshold (€1 million), a minimum export requirement (70 per cent of production) and the term of use of the facilities (five years), no clear reference is provided on the grounds and margins for accepting or refusing investors' entry.

Therefore, each zone can evaluate the investment projects based on its specific range of admission criteria. In the case of the Minsk FEZ, for instance, such criteria include the correspondence of the project to the "character of social and economic policy of the state", hardly a clear-cut criterion. Moreover, within each zone, the final entry decision is made by the Commission on the Promotion of Competitiveness of the Economy, composed of various representatives of the local and central government. These receive an admission evaluation report from the FEZ authorities, but have full discretional power to allow or refuse entry. Furthermore, their decisions cannot be appealed.

State support to foreign investment as set forth by the Investment Code

The code also provides for support by the state to foreign investors. This can take the form of: (a) guarantees of the Government of Belarus; (b) access to centralized investment resources; or (c) individual investment contracts with the state. A fourth form of support, in the area of tax and customs exemptions, was repealed in the latest revision of the code (and maintained only for investors signing individual investment contracts). Before giving this state support, the authorities put in place a complex examination (assessment) of the investment projects, based on the criteria provided for in the code.[35]

The first kind of support – the government guarantee – is available to lenders for the financing of investment projects.[36] Lenders include Belarusian legal entities or foreign states and their units, international organizations and foreign legal entities providing foreign currency loans to Belarus or to Belarusian legal entities.

Approval of such loans is based on a complex examination (assessment) of the candidate investment project, on the basis of a decision reached by the government as approved by the President.[37]

The Investment Code also provides for special government support for production based on new and advanced technologies.[38] The type, scope and duration of government support provided in this case are determined on a case-by-case basis by a decision of the President of Belarus. The support can be provided only to those organizations that are included in the list of industries and organizations using new and advanced technologies, as approved by the government.

---

[33] Law on Free Economic Zones 10.10.2008, Regulations on Free Economic Zones, Council of Ministers Resolutions, other laws, and acts of Administrations of Free Economic Zones.

[34] These include a business plan consisting of a résumé, the development strategy, the product description, the marketing strategy and production plan, the organizational plan, the investment plan, the legal plan and forecast of financial-economic activity, the technical-economic foundation and approval of the business location (the same as a guarantee letter). It shall also include information on the past activity of the business, the reference to volume of investments, average number of employees, average salary and production volume.

[35] Investment Code, articles 20 and 21.

[36] Ibid., articles 33.

[37] Ibid., chapter 6.

[38] Ibid., article 37.

The second kind of support – the centralized investment resources – is provided in the form of government funding for the financing of investment projects and Belarusian Government guarantees with regard to loans provided by Belarusian banks, upon condition that the investor's (national or foreign) own funds account for at least 20 per cent of the total investment. Based on the results of the review of investment projects, the Ministry of the Economy prepares a list of investment projects eligible for the allocation of centralized investment resources and submits the list within the framework of the annual Government Investment Programme for approval by the President of Belarus.

A third kind of support comes with the conclusion of an investment contract with the state.[39] This kind of agreement is put in place for investment projects with "significant importance to the economy of Belarus" and a minimum investment of $5 million.[40] The threshold may however be raised significantly in the near future. Access to investment contracts is possible for both foreign and domestic investors.

These agreements, typically in the form of rights and obligations for the two parties, the investor and the state (or subentity of the state), must respect a number of mandatory terms and conditions. An interesting feature is that they can contain additional legal guarantees offered by Belarus for the duration of the agreement. For instance, they can contain specific guarantees on the tax and customs regime applicable to the investor, the environmental standards, access to international arbitration and other issues of concern to the investor applicable at the date of the agreement, which would translate into some stabilization commitments on the part of the state. They may also include mutual obligations undertaken by the parties to develop the industrial and social infrastructure of the region, obligations to hire and train citizens of Belarus, the terms of the use of technologies as well as other terms, depending on the nature of the investment project.

Investment contracts pose a number of risks to the government as they offer tailored investment regimes to different investors. Currently, it is reported that only few such contracts exist, however, should the FDI inflows to Belarus increase as a result of a continued reform drive, it could become increasingly difficult for the authorities to keep track of them and monitor that the individual requirements set by these contracts are respected. Moreover, investment contracts risk creating arbitrariness in the conditions applying to similar investors, and put the government in a situation where it might be called upon its commitments by the investor at a later stage.

At the same time, investment contracts give latitude to the parties to negotiate special terms and conditions. They provide the government with a tool to attract strategic investments and investors with additional government guarantees. Therefore they constitute a powerful investment attraction instrument in a phase characterized by frequent and unpredictable legislative changes. Until the overall investment climate stabilizes, it is recommended that investment agreements be retained. However, one goal in improving the investment climate should be to standardize as much as possible the conditions applying under the individual investment agreements.

With the exception of this more flexible approach provided by the conclusion of investment agreements, the access to the guarantees and support given by the State of Belarus to foreign investment projects follows a strict and bureaucratic procedure that does not allow tailor-made conditions but at the same time does not exclude arbitrary refusals and non-transparent results in the decision-making process.

2.   Protection and treatment under the Investment Code

The provisions covering the protection and treatment of the foreign investor can be found in the general part of the code, alongside the general definitions. A standard range of treatment and protection is provided, but the content of each protection provision does not follow widely accepted international standards. This is however substantially compensated by a very extensive network of bilateral investment treaties (BITs) with many of the most important home countries of FDI.

---

[39]   Ibid., chapter 10.
[40]   Threshold determined by Council of Ministers Resolution 444 of 2002.

Under the code, foreign investors enjoy equal rights to all investors or economic actors engaged in investment activity for the duration of their investment, regardless of the form of ownership. However, as described in the competition section later in this chapter, the extent to which, in practice, the playing field is level for state-owned enterprises and private companies remains a major issue in Belarus.

No guarantee of fair and equitable treatment is offered, but the code provides that foreign investors and legal entities established with their participation shall not be treated less favourably than Belarusian legal entities and private individuals.[41] No significant exceptions to this rule could be identified in practice.

The former version of the code contained a stability clause according to which, "in the event that Belarusian legislation adopted subsequent to the creation of a commercial organization with foreign investment impairs the situation and business conditions for foreign investors and commercial organizations with foreign investment established with their participation (i.e. in the event that additional or increased obligations are imposed thereupon or in the event of a limitation or suppression of their rights), for a period of five years the legislation in effect at the date of registration of the commercial organization with foreign investment shall apply to the foreign investor, commercial organization with foreign investment, and/or foreign investments". This stability clause was repealed and currently applies solely to FEZ residents and only as regards their beneficial legal and tax regime. The effect of the stability clause is limited in time (seven years for FEZ residents registered after 1 April 2008 and until 31 March 2015 for FEZ residents registered before 1 April 2008). Also, the stability clause applies in full to investors in towns/settlements with a population under 50,000 people according to Presidential Decree 1 of 2008, as amended.

The code further guarantees the stability of the rights of investors to engage in and disengage from investment activity.

Transfer of funds. There is a guarantee for funds transfer, but it is not complete. It pertains only to the right to repatriate the post-tax profits (earnings) received in Belarus as a result of investment activity as well as the proceeds from the full or partial sale of invested assets upon termination of the investment activity. Article 97 of the code further states that the salaries of foreign employees (in commercial organizations with foreign investment) paid in foreign currency may be transferred abroad. Typically, an investment code would also guarantee transfer of compensation pursuant to expropriation; payments arising out of an investment dispute; payments made under a contract, including amortization of principal and accrued interest payments made pursuant to a loan agreement; and additional contributions to capital for the maintenance or development of an investment.

Protection against expropriation. According to Article 11 of the Investment Code, "nationalization and requisitioning shall only be possible subject to the timely and full compensation of the cost of the nationalized or requisitioned investment assets and other damages caused as a result of nationalization or requisition". Compensation includes interest (article 12). The code, however, is silent on the grounds for expropriation. Article 245 of the Civil Code of Belarus, on nationalization of property, is also vague on the grounds for expropriation, referring to conditions set forth in a specific law that has not been adopted as yet.

Access to courts and disputes settlement. The Investment Code does not contain a general guarantee for foreign investors to access national tribunals. However, the code grants foreign investors access to national courts in the following cases: (a) if an unlawful action (inaction) of government bodies and their officials infringes investors' rights or causes them loss or damage (article 13); (b) if state registration is denied (article 86); (c) to challenge the results of tenders and auctions in a concession (article 65); or (d) to appeal against the amount of compensation paid for a nationalized asset (article 12).

The Economic Procedural Code 219-3 of 1998, however, gives all legal entities access to the domestic economic tribunals, unless the legislation provides for "other administrative avenues" (article 6) to be explored.

The Investment Code does not contain a reference to any international arbitration mechanism. However, recourse to international arbitration is possible, according to the Economic Procedural Code, if included in a

---

[41]   Investment Code, article 79.

written agreement between two parties. This requires the mutual consent of the parties or the submission by the defendant in court of a motion to forward the dispute settlement to international arbitration.

One of the few examples of international arbitration between a foreign investor and a Belarusian investor is the dispute between the biggest Russian brewery OAO (otkrytoe aktsyonernoye obshchestvo or open joint-stock company) "Baltika" (part of the Baltic Beverage Holding) and the Belarus OAO "Krinica". The dispute was settled by the International Arbitration Court at the Russian Chamber of Commerce and Industry in 2004.[42]

Belarus became a member of the United Nations Commission on International Trade Law (UNCITRAL) in 2004 and actively cooperates with the organization. Belarus also signed the International Convention on the Settlement of Investment Disputes (ICSID) in 1992 and it entered into force in Belarus the same year. However, as mentioned, the Investment Code does not contain any reference to ICSID nor to the rights of investors to access international arbitration mechanisms. This is however a possibility provided for by the BITs of which Belarus is a signatory (see below). So far, no cases of disputes against Belarus have been brought under ICSID.

3.   The international framework for investment in Belarus

Belarus is one of the most active economies in transition in terms of the number of BITs concluded (figure II.1) having concluded, as of June 2008, 54 BITs (see annex I). The period between 1995 and 2001 witnessed a rapid growth of the BIT network with 32 agreements concluded. Forty-two per cent of the BITs concluded by Belarus are with developing countries and 41 per cent with capital-exporting developed countries. Only 17 per cent have been concluded with other economies in transition (figure II.2).

Figure II.1.   Number of BITs concluded by economies in transition, June 2008

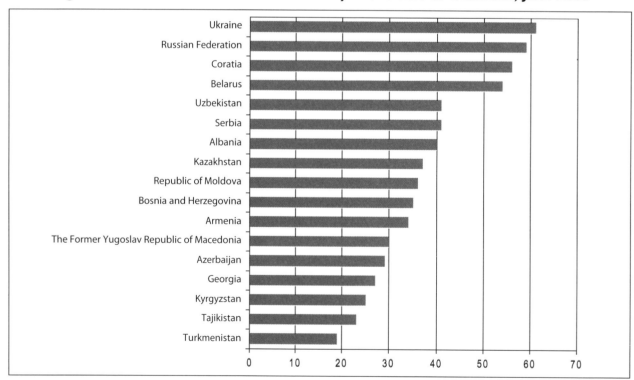

Source: UNCTAD.

---

[42] Up to 2001, 80.75 per cent of OAO "Krinica" belonged to the Belarusian State while the remainder was owned by the company's employees. In March 2001, an oral agreement was reached between the Belarusian authorities and the OAO "Baltika" for an investment by the latter of $50 million. In exchange, the Belarusian Government pledged to increase the founding capital of Krinica and give Baltika 51 per cent. Baltika started investing in the company but the Belarusian Government lowered Baltika's share to 30 per cent. As a result, Baltika reclaimed the invested funds. Finally, Krinica received a state loan to pay back Baltika.

About 80 per cent of the BITs concluded by Belarus have already entered into force. This is above the average rate of ratification of most developing countries and economies in transition. This may provide a positive signal to the international community that Belarus is serious about its international commitments on investment and its overall BIT strategy. However, some of the BITs were concluded more than 10 years ago and would require a legal review to ensure that the provisions still reflect the interests of the parties. Furthermore, this could also revive the momentum for the ratification process (e.g., the BIT with France, Pakistan and the United States).

Figure II.2. BITs concluded by Belarus by country groups, as of June 2008
(Percentage)

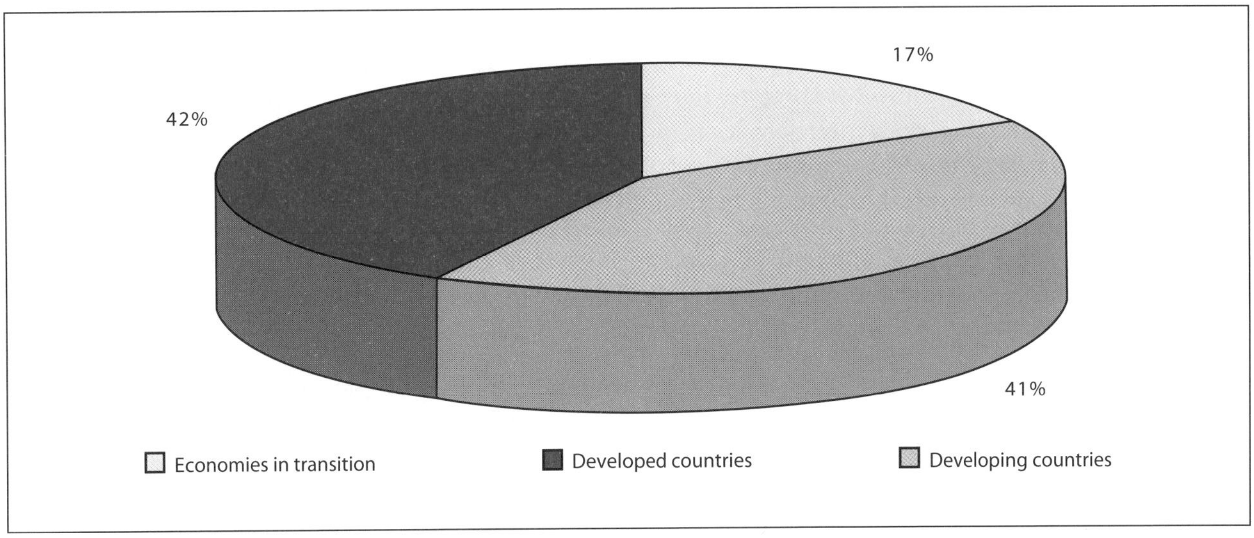

Source: UNCTAD.

Belarus relies primarily on BITs in its efforts to attract and protect FDI. Most internationally accepted treatment and protection standards are contained in the country's BITs (box II.2). According to available information, no free trade agreement concluded by Belarus includes investment protection chapters. The European Union still has not ratified the bilateral Partnership and Cooperation Agreement concluded in 1995.

Box II.2. Core elements of the BITs concluded by Belarus

Preamble. The preambles of the BITs concluded by Belarus often include language recognizing that the BIT will increase the prosperity and economic development of both states. The development dimension is strongly reflected in the BITs concluded with Finland and the Netherlands for example. The BIT with Finland recognizes the impact of the agreement on the economic development of the parties and clarifies that investment protection can be achieved without relaxing health, safety and environmental measures. The BIT with the Netherlands recognizes that the agreement will stimulate the flow of capital and technology between the parties.

Definition of investment. Investment is defined in a classical, broad, asset-based sense, covering movable and immovable property as well as any other rights such as mortgages, liens, pledges and similar rights. Investment also covers stock, shares, claims to money or to any performance having economic value. Intellectual property rights are also covered as a form of investment.

Promotion and protection of investment. Most of the BITs concluded by Belarus provide that the parties shall promote and admit foreign investment of the other party in accordance with its laws and regulations. Specific investment promotion measures are rarely included in the BITs concluded by Belarus.

Treatment of investments. The BITs concluded by Belarus provide for post-establishment most favoured nation treatment. However, the BIT concluded with Finland provide for pre-establishment rights, but only with regard to most favoured nation treatment. The BIT concluded with the United States, which also includes pre-establishment rights, was signed on 15 January 1994 but has not yet been ratified by the United States.

Expropriation. All the BITs concluded by Belarus protect investment against the risk of expropriation and nationalization. The BITs reviewed also covered measures having an effect equivalent to expropriation (indirect expropriation). In many BITs, it is clarified that compensation shall be equivalent to the market value of the expropriated investment at the time immediately before the expropriation. The London Interbank Offered Rate (LIBOR) rate is often used in the BITs by Belarus with regard to the interest due.

Transfers. Most of the BITs reviewed include a clause guaranteeing the free transfer of funds without any exceptions. However, some treaties include exceptions in the event of serious balance of payment difficulties or serious macroeconomic problems (e.g. the BIT with Slovakia). In some treaties, the parties can delay the free transfer of funds in a non-discriminatory manner to ensure that the investor has fulfilled its fiscal obligations (e.g. the BITs with Finland and the Islamic Republic of Iran).

Investor–state disputes. Most BITs give the investors the choice between the competent national courts of the parties, ICSID and UNCITRAL. The BIT with Pakistan also refers to the International Chamber of Commerce (ICC). The BIT with the Netherlands only provides for ICSID.

Source: UNCTAD.

4. Assessment and recommendations

The legal framework for investment in Belarus is open and contains only a few, standard sectoral restrictions. However, the decentralization of the investment registration and permitting process, matched with the possibility for the local levels of the administration to introduce secondary legislation regulating investors' entry has created scope for arbitrary refusals and non-transparent outcomes in the decision-making process. Increased investment attraction will require Belarus to augment the clarity, stability and predictability of its investment regime. Moreover, with respect to the treatment and protection of investors, the investment law has fallen behind the treatment and protection afforded under Belarus' international treaty provisions and under internationally accepted standards.

This review leads to the following three pillars for action:

a) Harmonize investors' treatment and protection to international standards

Whereas most protections generally afforded to foreign investors are covered in the Investment Code, the wording and the content of each of these provisions does not follow current international law standards or the actual BIT practice of the country. It is recommended that the Investment Code be reviewed to:

1. Offer protection provisions with respect to fair and equitable treatment and list the conditions under which the standard "not less favourable" treatment of foreign investors does not apply;
2. Introduce the conditions for expropriation to be considered lawful;
3. Guarantee the full range of funds transfer in accordance with the BITs' provisions;
4. Guarantee access to domestic and international dispute resolution mechanisms for foreign investors.

b) Harmonize the regional and national investment legislation

The inconsistencies between the Investment Code, the relevant presidential decrees and the instructions issued by the regional authorities in charge of state registration undermine the coherence, predictability and transparency of the FDI entry regime, essential elements of any FDI attraction policy. It is recommended that:

1. The investment legislation at all levels of government be harmonized with a view to ensuring consistency and avoiding unnecessary duplications in the state registration and other permitting processes;
2. The conditions for refusal of an investment project be detailed by the legislation so as to restrict the flexibility of local civil servants to assess the extent to which a project is valuable for the country on a case-by-case basis.

c) Strengthen the investment facilitation infrastructure

The decentralization of the investment registration and facilitation process to the regions poses potential issues regarding the consistent application of laws and regulations across the country. Even after the relevant legislation is harmonized, administrative capacity and expertise will differ widely from region to region. Attitudes towards private investors may vary as well. In such circumstances, it will be essential for the central government to ensure that laws and regulations are applied consistently and with a common understanding of the spirit of the Investment Code. The government is determined to set up a full-fledged national investment promotion agency (IPA) in the course of 2009. It is recommended that a phased approach is taken to:

1. Assign the new IPA a troubleshooting role between investors and the regions in the emergence of roadblocks to investment at the local level;
2. Assign the new IPA a primary role in providing assistance to the regions in the performance of their investment facilitation role, so as to enable all regions to attain the minimum required services standards;
3. Monitor and benchmark the performance of the different regions in investment facilitation with a view to helping them improve their administrative processes when dealing with investors and to fostering positive competition among them.[43]

B. General measures

1. Legal forms for business operation

The Belarusian legislation provides for a number of different legal forms through which businesses may operate in the country. Set out below is a brief description of those most relevant to foreign investors.

Representative offices

Representative offices were created to "investigate opportunities for investment, present the interests of an organization and perform representative and other functions" (article 51.1 of the Civil Code and Decree of the Council of Ministers 929 of 1997, as amended in November 2007). They are not regarded as legal entities and may not carry out business activities, unless this takes place on behalf and upon the authorization of the organization they represent. In practice, representative offices perform the functions of a branch as permanent establishments of a foreign legal entity.

Representative offices are created upon permission of the Ministry of Foreign Affairs, payment of an annual state duty[44] and presentation of a list of documents regarding the company and the purpose of its representative office. Under the Law on Income and Profit Taxes, representative offices become taxable only when they carry out commercial and other activities such as negotiating and signing contracts. Taxation of a commercial representative office is very similar to that of an ordinary Belarusian entity with minor distinctions.

---

[43] In this respect, Belarus could benefit from following the example of Viet Nam, which has introduced a Provincial Competitiveness Index based on survey data from business. Since the introduction of the index in 2005, many provinces have implemented new measures to streamline licensing and improving information for investors.

[44] The state duty for opening and extending the validity of an representative office's permit was around $1,060 as of April 2008.

Legal entities

According to the Investment Code (article 82), commercial organizations with foreign investment may open subsidiaries, affiliates and subsidiary unitary enterprises in accordance with the legislation of Belarus and that of the investor's country of origin. The three most common types of legal entities under the Belarusian Civil Code include joint-stock companies, limited liability companies and unitary enterprises. These are regulated by the Law on Business Entities and the Civil Code, respectively. The establishment of banks and insurance companies is regulated by separate legislative acts. Only joint-stock companies may issue shares and they are therefore subject to Belarusian securities law and the regulations imposed by the Department on Securities.

a.   Joint-stock companies

Joint-stock companies are those companies whose capital is divided into a definite number of shares. A joint-stock company may be either "open" or "closed". A joint-stock company is deemed open if its shares are distributed to the general public without the permission of other shareholders. It is closed if the distribution of its shares requires the consent of other shareholders, and/or shares are distributed only to certain categories of persons.

Open joint-stock company (otkrytoe aktsyonernoye obshchestvo, "OAO")

An OAO is the "supreme" type of company, permitting an unlimited number of shareholders. Subject to elaborate disclosure requirements, an OAO is the only form of legal entity whose shares may be openly traded. The minimum charter capital is set to an amount equivalent to €3,500.

Closed joint-stock company (zakrytoe aktsyonernoye obshchestvo, "ZAO")

The most common type of a joint-stock company is a ZAO. Shareholders enjoy pre-emption rights to any shares offered for sale by a retiring member. There is no obligation to publish accounts. The shares are distributed only among its founders or another predetermined group of persons. A ZAO may not hold an open subscription of shares for an unlimited group of people. The minimum charter capital of a ZAO is set at the rate equivalent to €900. The number of shareholders in the closed joint-stock company should not exceed 50.

b.   Limited liability company (obshchestvo s ogranichennoi otvetstvennostyu, "OOO")

An OOO is defined as a company founded by two or more persons, whose capital is divided into ownership interests, the amount of which is determined by statutory documents. Its capital is divided into "units", which are not technically shares and fall outside the scope of the Belarusian securities law. A drawback of an OOO with minority participants is that any participant has the right to withdraw from the company and is entitled to require other participants to purchase/redeem his or her units at pro rata value. The minimum charter fund of an OOO is not defined by legislation but the number of participants in the OOO should not exceed 50.

c.   Unitary enterprise

The unitary enterprise is defined as a commercial organization that has no ownership rights to the assets transferred to the company by the owner of these assets, which essentially means that such a company is not the owner of its property. Together with the OOO, the unitary enterprise is the most flexible type of company with the least onerous statutory obligations. Instead, the founder of such a company remains the owner of the assets. A unitary enterprise is liable for its obligations with all of the property belonging to it. A unitary enterprise does bear liability for the obligations of the owner of its property, except in the cases provided for in the Civil Code. The owner is also the founder of the company. These assets may not be divided into shares. A unitary company has only one founder and this, together with its simple management structure, often makes it the vehicle of choice for foreign investment.

2. Licensing

Further to the state registration procedure described in section A of this chapter, a large number of business activities require investors to obtain a licence. Licensing is perceived as one of the biggest administrative barriers for doing business in Belarus. Encouragingly, a recent presidential decree reduced the list of kinds of licensed activities (Presidential Decree 7 of 2007) from more than 150 to the 52 shown in box II.3 below. The decree also simplified and shortened the procedure for applying for and obtaining licences. However, many activities that do not pose public interest concerns still feature in the list. Also, in many cases, the lower levels of the administration have replaced licences with equally burdensome certification requirements.

Box II.3. Activities requiring a licence and issuing authority

Kind of activity	State bodies and state organizations carrying out the issue of special permits (licences)
1. Attorney activity	Ministry of Justice
2. Auditing activity	Minister of Finance, National Bank
3. Banking activity	National Bank
4. Game husbandry	Ministry of Forestry
5. Fish husbandry	Ministry of Agriculture and Food
6. Veterinary activity	Ministry of Agriculture and Food
7. Land surveying activity	State Committee on Property
8. Activity of temporary (anti-crisis) manager in procedure on insolvency (bankruptcy) case	Ministry of Economy
9. Activity in the sphere of aviation	Ministry of Transport and Communications
10. Activity in the sphere of industrial safety	Ministry of Emergency Situations
11. Activity in the sphere of communications	Ministry of Communication and Informatization
12. Activity in the sphere of customs affairs	State Customs Committee
13. Activity in the sphere of gambling business	Ministry of Sport and Tourism
14. Activity on wood harvesting and milling	Ministry of Forestry
15. Dealing with scrap and wastes of ferrous and non-ferrous metals	Ministry of Industry
16. Activity on securing the safety of legal and natural persons	Ministry of Internal Affairs
17. Activity on ensuring fire security	Ministry of Emergency Situations
18. Activity on organizing and holding electronic interactive games	Ministry of Finance
19. Security printing	Ministry of Finance
20. Activity on technical protection of information including by cryptography methods including application of electronic digital signature	State Centre of Information Security at the Operational and Analytical Centre
21. Dealing with precious metals and precious stones	Ministry of Finance
22. Activity connected with usage of natural resources and influence on environment	Ministry of Natural Resources and Protection of Environment

23. Activity connected with cryptographic protection of information and means of secret reception of information	Committee of State Security
24. Activity connected with the sale of narcotics and psychotropic substances and its precursors	Ministry of Health
25. Activity connected with the sale (except for retail trade, export and import) of alcohol, non-food alcohol containing products (except for antiseptic medicines and veterinary remedies that are non-food alcohol containing products), ethyl alcohol and tobacco goods	Regional Executive Committees and Minsk City Executive Committee
26. Activity connected with improving health of children abroad	Administrative Department of the President of the Republic of Belarus
27. Activity connected with conducting the control of radioactive contamination	Ministry of Emergency Situations
28. Activity connected with planting and growing the plants containing narcotic and poisonous substances	Ministry of Agriculture and Food
29. Activity connected with hiring in the Republic of Belarus foreign labour and employment of citizens of the Republic of Belarus abroad	Ministry of Internal Affairs
30. Activity connected with products for military purposes	State Military and Industrial Committee
31. Activity connected with production of alcohol (except for production of original alcoholic beverages in cultural and ethnographic centres, national parks and preserves of the Republic of Belarus with a view to recreate the fullness of Belarusian national traditions), non-food alcohol-containing products (except for antiseptic medicines and veterinary remedies that are non-food alcohol-containing products), non-food ethyl alcohol and tobacco goods	State Committee on Standardization
32. Activity connected with production of aluminium, lead, zinc, tin, cooper and casting of ready products and semi-products out of aluminium and hard non-ferrous metals	Ministry of Industry
33. Activity connected with service and civil weapons, ammunition for them, with collecting and exhibiting of weapons and ammunitions	Ministry of Internal Affairs
34. Activity connected with collection and dissemination (including in the global computer network Internet) of information about individuals with a view of their acquaintance	Ministry of Internal Affairs

35. Publishing activity	Ministry of Information
36. Lottery activity	Ministry of Finance
37. Medical activity	Ministry of Health
38. Educational activity	Ministry of Education
39. Rendering legal services	Ministry of Justice
40. Wholesale and retail trade of oil products	Belarusian State Concern on Oil and Chemistry
41. Activity in the sphere of automobile, inland waterway, sea transport (excluding inland transportation for own needs)	Ministry of Transport and Communication
42. Reprocessing and preserving fish and sea products	Administrative Department of the President of the Republic of Belarus
43. Printing activity	Ministry of Information
44. Projecting and construction of buildings and structures of I and II levels of responsibility and conducting of engineering pioneering for these purposes	Ministry of Architecture and Construction
45. Professional and stock exchange activity with securities	Ministry of Finance
46. Dissemination of legal information	Ministry of Justice
47. Retail trade (including alcohol drinks and tobacco goods) and catering	City (including in cities with district division) and Regional Executive Committees
48. Insurance activity	Ministry of Finance
49. Transport forwarding activity	Ministry of Transport and Communication
50. Tourist activity	Ministry of Sport and Tourism
51. Pharmaceutical activity	Ministry of Health
52. Private notary activity	Ministry of Justice

Source: Presidential Decree 17 of 2003, last amended on 6 October 2008.

Licences are issued by various state agencies, including ministries, state committees and departments as well as regional and city executive committees, upon presentation of a complete documentation package. Refusals from the authorities to issue a licence can be appealed in court. Presidential Decree 7 of 2007 reduced the number of documents needed to apply for a licence and introduced a declarative procedure for renewal. Quite importantly, the decree also determined that a state body is not allowed to request from investors documents that it can obtain itself from other state bodies. The term of the licence was also extended from 5 to 10 years and the list of reasons for revoking a licence became closed.

The President's initiative to reduce the number of licensed activities to about 50 is a welcome development. Nevertheless, many activities that require a licence are further divided into subtypes, bringing the total number of activities requiring a licence to around 400. Moreover, the initiative has met with a rearguard action by many government agencies, who have replaced the repealed licences with equally burdensome "certification" procedures. Another problematic feature of the current licensing regime is that the issuing bodies can revoke them even for minor violations without any court involvement. Since licences impose very detailed performance and operating conditions for an activity, violations occur frequently. The issuing authority can suspend the licence until the violations are eliminated or decide to suspend it for an indefinite period of time. Investors report that the first violation is generally sanctioned with an administrative fee, and the second with the removal of the licence.

The licensing requirements have become emblematic, within Belarus, of an overly bureaucratic approach to the regulation of economic activity. It is recommended that the licensing regime be further streamlined and reviewed to ensure that:

1. Licences are required only for those activities that pose potential public interest concerns with respect to health, safety or consumer protection. In this regard, licensing requirements for activities such as "printing", "publishing" and the "dissemination of legal information" should follow international practice;
2. The licence performance requirements are streamlined so as to protect the relevant public interest without imposing unnecessary restrictions on the licensed activity. This would also result in less frequent licence violations;
3. Repealed licences are not replaced on a systematic basis by equally burdensome certification requirements;
4. Appropriate appeal mechanisms are introduced in case a licence is revoked. This should include an administrative appeal and a judiciary one.

3. Taxation

The Belarusian tax system has for long been considered quite unattractive due to the number of taxes and procedures required to file and pay them.[45] In recent years, however, some improvements have been introduced. In particular, between 2005 and 2007, a total of 17 categories of taxes were eliminated and the authorities plan to continue reforming the system in the coming years. This section reviews the key elements of the fiscal regime affecting business.

Corporate taxpayers are subject to taxes levied by the state and the municipalities. The principal taxes for businesses in Belarus are the corporate tax ("profits tax"), which applies widely to trading income and gains on assets, land and the real estate levies, the environmental tax and local taxes and dues. The value added tax (VAT) applies but so also do a variety of sales taxes. Furthermore there are a number of ad hoc contributions such as the special contribution to the republican fund for support of food, agricultural producers and science organizations ("turnover tax") and the contributions to the innovation funds of various ministries.

A number of incentive schemes exist, aimed at supporting specific activities (agriculture, software and information technology (IT), export manufacturing) and the economic development of small cities and small enterprises. The key such incentives are presented in box II.4.

Corporate tax

The corporate tax rate is 24 per cent.[46] It applies to all businesses except for those eligible for incentive schemes (box II.4) and for activities that are tax exempt. Resident companies are taxed on their worldwide income but credit for foreign tax is available (including tax paid in non-treaty countries since January 2008). Non-resident companies are taxed on their income received in Belarus. The tax is levied on gross profit, which comprises the total profit from the sale of products, goods, services and other assets (including fixed assets and intangibles), property rights and income from non-sales operations, including gains on sales of securities less deductible expenses. Deductible expenses are standard items available in most tax codes. However, ceilings are established for the deduction of certain expenses such as information, consulting, advertising and marketing services (up to 7.5 per cent of the sales turnover).[47] As of 1 January 2009, such ceilings were abolished for such expenses as audit and personnel training. Also, interest is not directly deductible on loans used to acquire assets but is included in the depreciable value of the asset.

---

[45] See the World Bank Doing Business Report 2008.

[46] Equal to the Russian corporate tax rate, lower than Ukraine (25 per cent) but higher than in Latvia and Lithuania (15 per cent) and Poland (19 per cent).

[47] Special rules for the calculation of taxable income apply to banks and insurance companies.

Profit derived from the sale of baby food and the production of agricultural products is tax exempt. Profit reinvested in fixed assets for production purposes and housing construction is also exempt from corporate income tax.

Depreciable assets include a standard range of fixed assets as provided for in most tax codes. Depreciation is generally on a straight line basis. Intangibles can be amortized. The annual rates for the major groups are as follows:

- The cost of immovable property (such as buildings) can be depreciated at a rate ranging from 0.8 to 12.5 per cent;
- Plants, machinery and equipment from 3.3 to 20 per cent;
- Intangible property such as trademarks and patents, 5 to 10 per cent;
- Computers, 10 to 33.33 per cent;
- Transport vehicles from 2.5 to 25.55 per cent).

These rates of tax depreciation are very wide but this review has been unable to establish what rates are likely to apply in practice or whether the investor can choose which to apply. This is an important issue given that no carry forward of tax losses is currently permitted.

There is currently no carry-forward (or back) of losses (both ordinary and capital), and losses must be recognized in full in the year in which they are incurred. The authorities are however considering introducing some modifications in this area. If loss carry-forward is eventually permitted then it would be desirable to fix single rates for allowable depreciation. These would need to be at the highest end of the current ranges to accord with typical international practice.

The corporate tax, like other taxes, is paid monthly. This is highly unusual and adds to the paperwork for investors. The Belarusian authorities have examined the possibility of changing the tax filing and payment periods, and concluded that quarterly payment periods would be inadvisable. However, three payments per year in which the first two payments are based on estimates would represent a solution in line with practices in other countries.

Legal entities and individual entrepreneurs are also subject to a local transportation duty, which is applied to the net profits remaining after the collection of the corporate tax. In Minsk, the tax rate is 3 per cent (2 per cent of transportation duty and 1 per cent of infrastructure development duty). This is essentially another layer of corporate income tax.

Capital gains, withholding tax and income from securities

No separate capital gains tax is imposed and gains derived from the sale of property are taxable as normal business income. Gains from sales of securities are also subject to a rate of 24 per cent.

There is no withholding tax on dividends paid to residents. However such income adds to the recipient's taxable base for corporate tax purposes.

Dividends and royalties paid to non-residents are subject to a 15 per cent withholding tax, unless a treaty provides otherwise. Interest is imposed a 10 per cent final withholding tax on the gross amount, unless a treaty provides otherwise.

Belarus has signed double taxation treaties (DTTs) with 61 countries (as of 1 April 2009). They include all main countries source of FDI to Belarus, such as the Russian Federation, most EU countries and neighbouring Latvia, Poland and Ukraine. Many of them were concluded by the former Soviet Union. Treaties with major home countries of FDI provide significant relief on withholding taxes except in the case of the Russian Federation. For example, treaties with Austria, the Netherlands and the United Kingdom provide for withholding rates as low as 0 to 5 per cent on dividends, interest and royalties.

Personal income tax

The personal income tax rate is 12 per cent (flat rate). A 9 per cent flat rate applies to employment income of qualifying personnel of residents of the high technology parks and to the business income of individual entrepreneurs residents of the parks.

Indirect taxes and others

Value added tax

VAT is levied on the supply of the majority of goods and services and VAT registration is compulsory for businesses and individual entrepreneurs with a turnover in the three previous sequential months exceeding €40,000. The standard rate of VAT is 18 per cent. A zero rate applies to exports of goods and international transport services. A reduced rate of 10 per cent applies to domestic agricultural products and foodstuffs and certain other goods for children, in accordance with a list determined by the President. A reduced rate of 0.5 per cent rate applies to the import of diamonds and other precious stones from the Russian Federation for transformation purposes. A 24 per cent rate applies to sales and import of white sugar in Belarus. For goods and services subject to regulated prices, the VAT rates are 9.09 per cent and 15.25 per cent respectively.

The standard VAT payment period is one month and the VAT refund is reportedly speedy and efficient.

Land tax and corporate property tax

There is land tax levied in an annual lump sum amount per hectare of land. The tax is payable by the owners, lessees and users of land, with the exception of those benefiting from selected incentive schemes (box II.4). The tax rate is determined based on land value and depends therefore on its quality and location. For instance, in the city of Minsk, the land tax ranged, in 2008, from $360 to $7,000 per hectare (Ordinance of the President 365 of 2008). However, the Minsk City Council of Deputies and the Minsk City Executive Committee can increase or decrease the land tax rate, depending on the categories of payers or on the quality of location and infrastructure, though no more than twofold. The land payment rate is due regardless of the business performance of the landowner or user. The tax is deductible for corporate income tax purposes.

Until recently, all legal entities also paid an annual tax of 1 per cent on all immovable corporate property, i.e. buildings and other fixed assets excluding land and including construction in progress, that they either owned or rented. Since January 2009, only buildings and constructions (including in progress) are subject to this tax. During their first year in operation, buildings and other structures used by legal entities are exempted from this tax. Free zones and high technology park residents are also exempted from this tax with respect to property that is located directly in the zones or in high technology park territory. The corporate property tax is assessed and paid quarterly.

Environmental tax

An environmental tax ("ecological tax") is imposed on the discharge (release) of contaminants into the environment as well as on the volume of extracted natural resources and of processed oil and oil products. Different rates apply to volumes emitted or extracted and penalty multiples of 15 times apply to emissions over allowed limits. The environmental tax rate is determined by the President.[48]

Import and export duties

Duties are mostly ad valorem, but they may also be expressed as a set amount of euros per unit or kilogramme ("specified" duties), or as a combination of the two. Since 2001, there have been five ad valorem rates: 5, 10, 15, 20 and 25 per cent. Certain goods could be imported duty free. The weighted average tariff is only 11 per cent.[49]

---

[48] This review has been unable to discern the basis for the ecological tax rates. Investors say that the rates were burdensome until they were amended in May 2007 and again in September 2008.

[49] As of January 2008, there has been some revision of product goods to which these tariffs apply as part of preparation for an application to join the WTO but details of the impact on weighted average tariffs are not available.

The application of duties may vary, however, depending on the country of origin of the goods. Countries are classified into three groups for the purposes of charging import duties:

Group	Duty
Free trade nations	Exempt from import duties
Preferred nations (nations with "favourable conditions")	Basic rates of duty apply
Non-preferred trading nations	Double the basic rate

As Belarus is a member of the EurAsEC (Eurasian Economic Community) free trade area, exports and imports between these countries are generally exempt from customs duties (box 1.1). Also, goods originating from countries in the CIS are not subject to import duties. There is currently no list of non-preferred trading nations. Double the basic duty rate applies to goods originating from countries with which the Republic of Belarus has no mutual contractual obligations to provide a not less favourable regime. If the country of origin of the goods cannot be identified, the basic rate applies, unless the customs authorities find evidence that the country of origin has no mutual contractual obligation to apply the most favoured nation regime to the Republic of Belarus.

A limited number of goods, e.g. fuels and marine products, exported outside the borders of EurAsEC are subject to export duties.

Special customs regimes apply that provide import duty relief on goods to be further processed for export and apply import duty only on the value added abroad of Belarusian products that are reimported.

Turnover, sales and services taxes

Until 2007, a turnover tax of 3 per cent from the sales of goods, works and services contributed to the "republican fund for support of food, agricultural production and science organizations". Also, a "road user's fund" was in place, levied at 1 per cent of the turnover of sales of goods and services, and collected together with the turnover tax (Law 191-3 of 2006). Since 1 January 2008, the road user's fund has been abolished and the turnover tax was reduced to 2 per cent. The authorities again lowered the turnover tax to 1 per cent in January 2009, and plan to abandon it altogether in 2010.

Local authorities have numerous tax powers that can affect business. The most significant ones are the sales tax and the services tax. A tax on sales value is payable in certain municipalities where the retail trade takes place. A services tax applies for the following kinds of services: markets (fairs), hotel services, restaurant services, mobile telecommunication services for telephone subscribers, individuals' car maintenance and repair services and various entertainment services. Since 1 January 2009, a single rate of 5 per cent was set for both the local sales and services taxes. The authorities are considering the possible abolishment of the local sales tax in 2010.

Both sales and services taxes are of wide application and it is very unusual for such taxes to apply in conjunction with a VAT regime. These "flat taxes" (sales and services taxes) could significantly increase the effective tax burden on investment to the extent that the incidence of these taxes falls on business and not on the consumer. UNCTAD's tax model was used to assess the potential burden on business of the sales and services taxes, as measured by the discounted present value of taxes paid as a percentage of pre-tax cash flow (see annex 2 for details of UNCTAD's tax model).[50] In both manufacturing and services, the flat taxes approximately double the tax burden on business arising from corporate taxation alone, when the full tax burden is passed back to the producer.

---

[50] The model results assume that the turnover tax will be phased out and eventually eliminated as planned in 2010.

Other taxes on business

A 0.2 per cent registration duty is payable upon the registration of shares with the Securities Committee, where such a registration obligation exists. The total amount of the registration duty should not exceed 300 base value.

Belarus has a system of ministerial "innovation funds", which in many cases are simply additional contributions to the operational costs of ministries. For instance, since 2008, all entities engaged in wholesale and retail sale must contribute 0.25 per cent (or more in some cases) of their turnover to the innovation fund of the Ministry of Trade. Wholesalers of oil products contribute 1.5 per cent of turnover to this innovation fund. The Ministry of Architecture and Construction collects 1.35 per cent of the value of works under construction, with some exemptions. Other ministries and governmental bodies are also entitled to establish such innovation funds.

Telecommunications operators contribute 1.5 per cent of their annual profits to a universal access fund but these, more appropriately, are dedicated to providing services to lower-income citizens.

As shown below, the corporate tax burden can be significantly reduced by various incentives for investment in priority industries, especially high technology industries that are based in or given a status of high technology park, export manufacturing industries located in FEZs and rural areas (box II.4).

Box II.4. Key fiscal incentives in Belarus

High technology activities

In general, profits derived from the production of high technology goods and services are subject to corporate income tax at a reduced rate of 10 per cent. Moreover, companies engaged in the analysis, design and software support of information systems, software-based data processing and similar activities are eligible to become residents of a high technology park. Even though Presidential Decree 12 of 2005 specifically determines the size and location of the land to accommodate the high technology park, it seems that at present location within the park is not a requirement to be eligible for the incentive. Once investors obtain a certificate proving they are part of the technology park and provided they pay 1 per cent of their gross income to the park administration, they are eligible for certain fiscal incentives, valid for 15 years (as per Presidential Decree 12 of 2005). These include:

1. Exemption from taxes, duties and obligatory payments envisaged by the Law on Budget, such as the contributions to innovation funds;
2. Exemption from corporate tax, import duties on goods immediately related to their activity and VAT;
3. Exemption from social insurance tax within the limits of "one average salary";
4. Exemption from taxes on land and immovable property;
5. Exemption from taxes on construction;
6. Employment income for employees taxed at a 9 per cent rate;
7. Withholding tax rate for dividends, interest, royalties paid to foreign legal entities of 5 per cent;
8. No offshore duty;
9. Fifty per cent discount on rental rates for industrial premises (Presidential Edict 495 of 2002).

Continues on next page...

Free economic zones

Residents in the six free economic zones enjoy a special tax and customs regime, as per Presidential Edict 262 of 2005 and as amended by Presidential Edict 42 of 2008. These include:

1. Exemption from customs duties and zero-rated VAT on all imported goods used to produce exports;
2. Exemption from customs duties and VAT if the goods produced in the zone are sold on the domestic market, provided that the goods are included in the "import substitution list" (i.e. a list of goods not produced in Belarus);
3. Exemption from corporate tax for five years after establishment with respect to the profits derived from the sale of own products* or services, and corporate tax reduced by 50 per cent in the following years;
4. Deduction from taxable income for profits reinvested in Belarus (except in the Brest FEZ);
5. VAT reduced by 50 per cent on sale of own products in Belarus;
6. Exemption from turnover tax, contribution to innovation funds, real estate tax, tax on the acquisition of motor vehicles and payroll tax (these apply with respect to the sale of own products to foreign legal entities and individuals, the sale of own products in Belarus if the products are included in the import substitution list and the sale of own products to other zone residents);
7. Five years' tax stability guarantee.

Small business

Small business, with some exceptions, can choose to adopt a "simplified taxation system" that replaces the general tax system with one tax levied on gross revenues. According to Presidential Decree 119 of 2007, these are:

1. Microentities: companies with a number of employees not exceeding 15 persons and revenue for the first nine months of the year not exceeding BYR 1 billion, corresponding to around $350,000. These are subject to tax at a rate of 8 per cent on their gross revenue and are exempted from any other tax including VAT, except for taxes and duties on imports, state fees, offshore duty, registration and licensing fees, vehicle acquisition tax and social security contributions;
2. Other small companies: companies with a number of employees not exceeding 100 persons and revenue for the first nine months of the year not exceeding BYR 3.5 billion, corresponding to around $1.3 million (small entities). These are subject to tax at a rate of 6 per cent of their gross revenue and are exempted from the same taxes as the microentities, with the exception of VAT, which they have to pay.

Agricultural producers

Companies for whom more than 50 per cent of turnover is generated by the production and sales of agricultural products are eligible to pay a unified tax of 2 per cent on the gross revenues from sales of goods (works, services) and other property and income earned on non-operating transactions (Presidential Edict 27 of 1999). Companies opting for the unified tax system are exempted from the payment of the corporate tax and most other taxes excluding VAT, import taxes and payroll contributions.

Continues on next page...

Individual entrepreneurs

Individual entrepreneurs can opt for one of three regimes: the common system of taxation (with rates from 9 to 30 per cent), the simplified taxation system or the single tax for individual entrepreneurs.

Companies established in rural areas

Entities and individual entrepreneurs residing in those localities that have been reconstructed in "agro-towns" (according to the State Programme of Countryside Renewal and Development for 2005–2010) or companies establishing business activities in cities with a population under 50,000 inhabitants are eligible for an incentive regime (Presidential Edict 1 of 2008), as follows:

1. Five years' exemption from corporate tax on sales of own products and services and the tax contributing to the Republican Fund for Support of Manufacturers of Agricultural Products, Foodstuffs and for Agrarian Science;
2. No customs duties and no VAT on machinery and equipment used as founding capital of the company.

Also, companies and individual entrepreneurs residing in rural areas are exempt from the corporate tax and the tax on immovable property from 1 January 2008 until 31 December 2012, if they provide goods, perform works or render services in rural settlements (Presidential Decree 9 of 2007).

Individual investment contracts

Investors with projects of "significant importance to the economy of Belarus" and a minimum investment of $5 million are eligible to conclude individual investment contracts with the state. These can contain additional legal guarantees for the duration of the agreement with regard to the tax and customs regime, environmental standards and other issues, which would translate into some stabilization commitments on the part of the state. They may also include mutual obligations undertaken by the parties to develop the industrial and social infrastructure of the region, the investor's right to export from Belarus goods and profit (income) resulting from the implementation of the investment agreement, obligations to hire and train citizens of Belarus, the terms of the use of technologies as well as other terms, depending on the nature of the investment project.

Source: UNCTAD.

* "Own" products is not defined but is presumed to mean products with a degree of value added by the seller.

Interviews carried out by UNCTAD for the purpose of this review indicate that the incentive schemes are appreciated by business primarily because they reduce the number of taxes and therefore the procedures involved in paying them. This is particularly true for the high technology and free zones schemes. The simplified taxation system for small business goes in the same direction but it is not, in certain circumstances, an attractive scheme in terms of the actual tax burden imposed on SMEs. According to UNCTAD's tax model, this depends principally on whether a sales or services tax would otherwise apply. For example, in services, the simplified taxation system is more favourable than the general tax regime only for those activities to which the services tax of 10 per cent applies. In these cases, the simplified system imposes a burden comparable to the general tax regime because it eliminates the services tax. In all other services, the tax burden is lower under the general regime than under the simplified taxation system. Similarly, the simplified taxation system reduces the overall tax burden for a manufacturing firm only if a sales tax would otherwise apply.

With respect to the specifics of the free zones incentive scheme, there is a possibility for manufacturers on the "import substitution list" to import inputs free of duty and be exempted from VAT if the goods produced in the FEZ are sold on the domestic market. This is problematic as it constitutes a double incentive that discriminates among producers in Belarus and risks creating a very uncompetitive manufacturing sector in the zones.

Assessment of taxation

In conclusion, Belarus has started reforming its fiscal regime to make it more competitive for both local and foreign investors. The reduction and planned abolition of the turnover tax and the introduction of simplified taxation schemes for small businesses and individual entrepreneurs are two encouraging examples. Belarus' fiscal competitiveness is nevertheless held back by the existence of multiple flat taxes based on sales introduced at the local level, by ad hoc contributions to the various innovation funds of the public administration and by the complexity that tax reporting and payment imposes on business.

This review leads to several main recommendations on re-orienting tax policy to better serve Belarusian investment and development objectives:

- The general rate of corporate taxation is not overly burdensome. The overall tax burden would however be more adequate if the higher rates of allowable depreciation were applied. In this regard, Belarus should consider introducing loss carry-forward so as to avoid offsetting the value of the depreciation allowances. Thus, it is recommended to establish the loss carry-forward for at least five years and to fix the capital depreciation rates at the highest end of the current ranges;

- The sales and services taxes introduced by the local authorities should be abolished altogether. Belarus already has a working VAT system with an adequate rate. Adding other kinds of flat taxes make the overall taxation of business in Belarus uncompetitive compared to neighbouring countries. In this regard, the gradual elimination of the turnover tax – another form of flat tax – is a welcome reform. Where necessary, the authorities should consider compensating the loss in fiscal revenues to the local administrations by reviewing the redistribution mechanism of central government revenues and by ensuring an adequate fee structure for the provision of local services;

- When innovation funds and other ad hoc contributions constitute additional funds to cover the operational costs of ministries, they should be replaced by "payments for services offered" or devoted to specific developmental outcomes (such as the current innovation fund for telecommunications);

- The simplified taxation system for small business is helpful for reducing the administrative requirements related to paying taxes. However, if the sales and services taxes were abolished (as recommended), the current rates under the simplified system would need to be reduced so that small businesses do not pay a disproportionate amount of taxes. In these circumstances, UNCTAD estimates that the rates of simplified tax should be halved;

- The simplification of the tax filing and payment system should continue. While the planned electronic payments system is encouraging, the monthly payments of the corporate tax and other taxes could be effectively replaced by three payments per year (with the first two payments being based on estimates);

- In an effort to sustain FDI attraction from key emerging investors such as Latvia and Poland, the treaty withholding rates applicable to those countries should be harmonized with those applicable to Belarus' traditional investors (ranging from 0 to 5 per cent);

- The incentives for free zones producers of goods under the import substitution list create discrimination among local producers and distortions in the allocation of productive resources. They should be reviewed to better match the development objectives of the government.

4.   Foreign exchange arrangements

The key provisions regarding foreign exchange arrangements in Belarus are Law 226-3 of 2003 Concerning Foreign Currency Regulation and Foreign Currency Control and the two resolutions of the National Bank of Belarus (204 of 1997 and 72 of 2004). Based on these, no permits or licences are required for current account currency transactions between residents and non-residents. In addition and since November 2001, Belarus has accepted the provisions of the International Monetary Fund (IMF) Agreement article VIII that require the exchange rate to be free of restrictions on payments and transfers for current account transactions.

As mentioned in part A of this chapter, the Investment Code (section 1, chapter 3, articles 10, 92, 94, 96) clearly states that foreign investors may at their sole discretion dispose of income or revenue generated as a result of investment activities, including reinvesting in the Republic of Belarus.

Foreign investors can open accounts in Belarusian roubles and foreign currency. However, several restrictions in the foreign exchange regime remain. Presidential Edict 452 of 2006 obliges all legal entities and entrepreneurs to the mandatory conversion of 30 per cent of their foreign currency earnings into Belarusian roubles. Companies registered and operating in cities with a population of less than 50,000 people, residents of a high technology park and residents of FEZs are exempt from this requirement, as well as a long list of other companies contained in the law (Presidential Decrees 1 of 2008 and 42 of 2008). Indeed, it appears that few companies are still subject to this requirement. However, it can be especially harmful to many service providers whose operational costs are not necessarily high and where such an obligation could lead to losses. In this regard, the authorities might want to review the need for such a mandatory conversion and explore alternative measures.

Another restriction deals with import/export operations, where each contract resulting in a currency payment of more than €3,000 has to be supplemented by a so-called "contract passport". Earlier, import/ export contracts were registered and monitored by customs officials. This was changed in 2008 by Presidential Edict 178, which transferred the registration and monitoring functions regarding such contracts to banks. According to the authorities, contract passports serve mainly as statistical monitoring instruments. Both government officials and business representatives confirm that such contract passports do not pose a significant obstacle, as they remain a simple registration requirement. It should be noted, however, that the €3,000 ceiling is very low. Undoubtedly it is an extra burden for both banks and entrepreneurs and the authorities should consider its repeal or, at least, an increase in the applicable threshold.

A more cumbersome restriction is contained in Edict 178 of 2008, according to which payments for goods/services in an export contract must be received within 90 days after shipment. In import operations, goods must be received not later than 60 days after payment. This is problematic for business, as it is often the case that export contracts have a much more elaborated payment system going well beyond the limits of 60 or 90 days. For such cases, a special justified request to the National Bank of Belarus is needed, providing detailed information regarding the deal's parameters. This is one example where rules that are too stringent generate unnecessary efforts for all parties involved.

Finally, in order to open foreign accounts abroad, residents need a permit from the National Bank of Belarus. Authorization is given on a case-by-case basis and depends on a number of criteria including the type of activity and the nature of the investment (the documentation requested differs according to whether the accounts are needed for portfolio investment or for FDI and can also differ based on the request).

In summary, the Belarusian foreign exchange system is sophisticated and operational. Both authorities and business representatives agree that it does not pose major challenges or obstacles for doing business. However, several restrictions remain that would require a re-evaluation so as to better protect the public interest. In particular, it is recommended that:

- The obligatory conversion of 30 per cent of the hard currency earned by legal entities and entrepreneurs in Belarus be reviewed;
- The time limits for the receipt of goods/payments in import/export operations be increased. A simplification that allows companies to pay or receive payments within 12 months (with a possible ceiling on the amount) would still offer sufficient control leverage to the authorities while significantly simplifying the system;
- The need to obtain a passport for each import/exports contract exceeding €3,000 should be reconsidered.

5. Labour

The labour regime in Belarus is based on the Labour Code of 1999 and the rules for its application. The code has been frequently amended and the latest revision available for this review is that of December 2007.[51] Labour market regulations present a mix of flexibility in hiring and firing procedures, high social contributions but low wage rates and significant rigidities in the wage-setting process.

Employers are required to provide their employees with social security, a minimum paid holiday period of 21 days per year, and double wage or extra vacation days in compensation for overtime (which should not exceed four hours in two consecutive work days and 120 hours per year). The social insurance, which also covers sickness, maternity benefits, work injury and family allowances, is financed through a contribution of 35 per cent of payroll by the employer[52] and 1 per cent by the employee. As shown in table II.1, social security contributions are higher in Belarus than in all other neighbouring countries. However, low wages compensate for these high social contributions.

Table II.1. Social security contributions

Country	Employer rate as % of employees' wages
Belarus	35
Latvia	24.09
Lithuania	23.6
Poland	9.76
Russian Federation	20
Ukraine	32.3

Source: United States Social Security Administration (2007).

A rigid wage determination process is in place, which effectively prohibits a free interplay between entrepreneurs and labour in setting wages. The minimum wage (determined annually by the Ministry of Labour and Social Protection) was BYR 208,800 in January 2008 (Council of Ministers Resolution 111 of 2008). This corresponds to approximately $100 per month while the average wage is of around $500 per month. Apart from the minimum wage, a single tariff system sets a series of 27 qualification grades and their corresponding salary coefficients. In addition, a series of specific factors are to be considered such as job position, industry field, rank and number of years in employment.[53] Investors must comply with very specific legal requirements in order to increase the offered wage according to criteria that vary by industry field, technical qualifications and complexity of the job performed. Moreover, according to the system, the largest possible difference between the lowest paid (grade 1) and the best paid (grade 27) is 7.84 times. Therefore, if grade 1 corresponds to the minimal wage then assumingly grade 27 would be approximately $784.

---

[51] Including Law 296-3 of 1999, Law 37-3 of 2005, Law 118-3 of 2006, Law 138-3 of 2006, Law 219-3 of 2007, Law 272-3 of 2007 and Law 299-3 of 2007.
[52] This is the general rate, although it can be lower according to the type of industry and type of enterprise.
[53] Ministry of Labour and Social Protection Resolution 2 of 2001, amended by Ministry of Labour and Social Protection Resolution 41 of 2008.

From the point of view of foreign investors (and of business in general), this system is overly complicated, rigid to administer and leads to mistakes. Furthermore, the economic rationale behind such a system can also be questioned. Its rigidity is likely to reduce a manager's ability to set wages so as to attract talent to the company. Moreover, TNCs generally maintain foreign managers at the head of their subsidiaries, at least during the first years after establishment. The cap on the maximum retribution poses therefore significant challenges in attracting the best managers to Belarus. The problem is not limited to the managerial level. Belarus also faces a drain of technical and skilled workers in various sectors, who are attracted by higher wages offered in the Russian Federation and other neighbouring countries. In this regard, the state's role in wage-setting should be limited to establishing minimum wages so as to protect the lowest paid and, together with the trade unions, guarantee that employee rights are protected, while fostering rules and principles guaranteeing adequate returns on labour at all levels.

All employment is by written contract. Collective work agreements exist for various categories of workers. The Labour Code sets five basic types of work contracts:

1. Indefinite duration;
2. Fixed term of one to five years;
3. Specific task/work-related;
4. Substitution for employee on a temporary leave of absence;
5. Seasonal work.

A fixed term contract of one year is the most common contractual arrangement used by foreign investors. This is likely due to the difficulties for the employer to terminate an indefinite duration contract. Importantly though, if a fixed term contract is not renewed but the employee continues performing the work, such a contract is automatically converted into an indefinite duration contract.

Indeed, the article 42 of the Labour Code defines precise conditions for the termination of a work contract by the employer. These apply both to indefinite and fixed term contracts. An employee may be fired only for "serious violations" (e.g. theft or alcoholism) or "systemic failure to handle the work responsibilities" and "only when being previously reprimanded". However the code also contains provisions with respect to trial periods and downsizing. The trial period for new employees (article 28) can be up to three months and allows the employer to evaluate the qualifications, motivation and suitability of the new employee. The scope of its application is, however, seriously restricted as trial periods are forbidden for:

- Young workers after graduation from professional schools;
- Young specialists after graduation from universities or colleges;
- Moving from one employer to another.

In case of company downsizing, no special permissions are needed to lay off employees other than informing the trade unions with two weeks' advance notice (article 46). Again, limitations apply. It is not possible, for instance, to retrench employees if they can be given another job in the company, even if this would require additional training (article 43). The code also indicates which workers should be preferred over others in case of downsizing (artcile 45): those with better productivity and qualifications. This, however, is left to managers' discernment.

Termination of an indefinite work contract by the employee is easier and requires a simple notification to the employer with one month's notice (article 40). However, it is difficult for the employee to terminate a fixed term contract. The main reasons defined by the code are health problems and/or disability or violations of labour legislation by the employer. No termination upon notice is therefore possible for fixed term contracts.

According to article 48 of the Labour Code, an employee is entitled to severance pay in an amount that depends on the motive for the termination of the contract. In case of termination for a serious violation of the labour code by the employee, no severance pay is due. However, two months' notice must be given or payment made in lieu of notice. Termination in the case of liquidation of the employer's organization is compensated by three months' average wage. Dismissal due to the reduction in the number of employees or staff positions is connected with a number of additional guarantees, such as increased amount of dismissal pay, leave entitlement and others. The amount of severance pay can be increased taking into account the length of service or other grounds provided by collective agreements.

Collective labour disputes are regulated by chapter 36 of the Labour Code, which provides for a standard range of dispute settlement mechanisms. In case of discontent with the conditions of a given collective work agreement, the employees' list of demands must be approved by a meeting representing no less than half the employees. Three days after receiving the workers' demands, employers are obliged to inform the Republican Labour Arbitration body and the employees about their decision. Partial or full rejection of the demands leads to the creation of a reconciliatory commission or resort to a mediator. If that does not help, the sides may seek labour arbitration by mutual agreement. The arbitrator's decision does not have obligatory character (unless the two sides agree otherwise). In case the parties are not satisfied with the arbitrator's decision, they may address the Republican Labour Arbitration body. The latter must make a decision within two weeks after being addressed and in most cases its decisions are binding.

The right to strike is also guaranteed in the legislation to all but government officials. Strikes can only take place if no less than two thirds of the participants agree in a secret vote. The employer should be notified about the strike at least two weeks in advance. The strike must take place within three months from the time the reconciliatory commission's suggestions (or those of the mediator or non-obligatory work arbitration) were rejected. Government officials interviewed during this review reported that no strike has taken place in Belarus for over six years.

The main internationally recognized labour standards are also guaranteed in national legislation and the country has ratified 49 International Labour Organization (ILO) conventions, including the eight core ones. Nevertheless, the International Confederation of Free Trade Unions, the European Trade Union Confederation and the World Confederation of Labour have all raised concerns over the treatment of trade unions in the country, reporting government interference in their activities and violation of trade union rights.[54] In 2003, the ILO set up a special enquiry commission that analysed the observance of the ILO Freedom of Association and Protection of the Right to Organize Convention and the Right to Organize and Collective Bargaining Convention. As a result, on 8 June 2007, Belarus was included for the fifth time in the special paragraph of the International Labour Conference Report as a country where rights of trade unions were violated. In the same month, the European Union excluded Belarus from the EU General System of Preferences for violation of rights of trade unions. According to the International Trade Union Confederation, while the government has taken some steps in the right direction, anti-union practice still remained firmly in place in 2008.[55] It should be noted, however, that the measures taken by the government to address the ILO recommendations at the International Labour Conference of 2008 resulted in the country being cleared from the special paragraph, for the first time since 2001.

Key recommendations are for the government to:

- Introduce more flexible wage-setting regulations. The current system does not allow investors to attract and reward managers and employees based on their skills and productivity. It is recommended

---

[54] Among the complaints figured the following: adoption and promulgation of anti-union legislation and executive decrees; refusal of registration of union organizations; harassment and threats, including threats of physical abuse; arbitrary transfers of union leaders, members and/or activists; forced resignation by workers from their union membership; freezing of unions' bank accounts; and denial of the rights of national workers' organizations to take part in statutory meetings of national tripartite labour institutions.
[55] International Trade Union Confederation (ITUC) (2008).

that the wage classification system be revised so as to protect the lowest paid workers by introducing different minimum wage levels for different categories of workers, while allowing entrepreneurs to freely set wages above the minimum levels;

- Continue cooperation with social partners and the ILO regarding the observation of trade union rights and freedom of association. Not only would this improve the protection of workers in the country and the status of industrial relations, but it would also positively affect the FDI attractiveness of Belarus. Western TNCs are indeed becoming increasingly receptive to transnational advocacy networks and to pressure from their home country governments, trade unions and customers, who are requesting from them more socially responsible behaviour;
- Consider introducing the possibility for employees to terminate fixed term contracts upon provision of sufficient notice, in accordance with international good practice.

6. Employment and residence of non-citizens

The key legislation regulating the employment and residence of non-citizens in Belarus includes: the Law of the Republic of Belarus on Legal Status of Foreign Citizens and Stateless Persons in the Territory of the Republic of Belarus of June 1993 (last amended in July 2005); the Law on External Labour Migration of July 1998; Presidential Decree 17 of 2003 on Licensing of Specific Types of Activities; the Council of Ministers Resolution 73 of January 2006 on Adoption of the Rules of Stay of Foreign Citizens and Stateless Persons in the Republic of Belarus; and the Council of Ministers Resolution 144 of February 2006 on Adoption of the Order of Issuing Residence Permits for Foreigners and People with No Citizenship. The legislation makes it possible to hire foreign managers and workers.

In general, any company wishing to hire foreign labour in Belarus must apply for a licence from the Ministry of Internal Affairs. Before soliciting the licence at the national level, however, investors must receive preliminary approval from the Department of Internal Affairs at the regional level. This review was unable to identify the criteria adopted at the regional level to assess licence applications. The request for the licence should set out the reasons for foreign hire and specify how many foreign positions are needed, the country of origin of the foreign workers considered necessary, their field of activity and copies of their draft work contract. Licences should be issued within one month, for a fee of approximately $140. They are valid for five years and can be renewed by repeating the application procedure.

Upon receipt of the licence, the employer needs to obtain a work permit for each foreign employee from the Administration of Citizenship and Migration of the Regional Executive Committee. The relevant request is accompanied by information concerning the worker and a copy of the employer's licence. The decision on the issuance of the work permit is taken after the employer solicits and receives a positive opinion from the Regional Labour Agency, also placed within the Regional Executive Committee. This opinion, to be issued within five days, is based on the satisfaction of a labour market test (i.e. if the authorities consider that the job to be performed by the foreign worker cannot be efficiently performed by Belarusian nationals). The working permit is valid for one year and can be renewed.

The employee who has been assigned the permit requests an entry visa through the representative office of the Ministry of Foreign Affairs. Once in Belarus, the employee needs to request a residence permit from the regional office of the Ministry of Internal Affairs. This is also valid for one year, renewable. Renewal requires a formal request to the ministry and is issued in about 10 working days. The procedure for employees of FEZs or high technology parks is the same.

As of 2009, foreign investors are able to employ founders and directors without having to receive a licence (Law 354 of July 2008). Also, no licence is needed to hire Russian citizens. The individuals concerned, of course, must still have the necessary work permits as per the procedure described above. Similar provisions are envisaged for representative offices of foreign companies as well as companies located in

FEZs. Representative offices are entitled to employ up to three foreign managers. Foreigners who invest a minimum of €150,000 or who are responsible for implementing particular government programmes also have the right to obtain residence permits.

The regime for the entry of foreign managers and investors is liberal but the procedure for hiring foreign workers is cumbersome, involves an excessive number of authorizing bodies and the allocation of work permits is not guaranteed, even after investors have passed the licensing stage. The recent revision of the law on the hiring of foreign directors and founders is a step in the right direction and will facilitate the key foreign personnel requirements of foreign investors. Belarus could find it extremely beneficial to attract foreign skills through FDI and should make this an explicit objective of its FDI policy. To this end, the foreign workers' entry regime could be streamlined and revised as follows:

- A one-stop approach to the expatriate entry process could be adopted, whereby investors would deal with one interface of the public administration and their requests would be internally processed and communicated by the various departments (Ministry of Internal Affairs, Ministry of Labour and Ministry of Foreign Affairs);
- The labour market testing procedure should be replaced, at least for high-skill positions and jobs, with an Australian-type approach whereby a predetermined list of skills shortages is drawn up. With appropriate safeguards, investors seeking foreign employees of those kinds would not need to await the results of the labour market testing to hire foreign workers;
- The work and residence permit should be merged, according to internationally accepted practice. This in itself would greatly reduce administrative procedures;
- The validity of the work and residence permit should be extended to five years renewable for the founders and directors of the foreign company and to three years for others.

7. Land

Until a proper market for land develops, access to land remains probably the single largest obstacle facing investors willing to establish in Belarus. The availability and accessibility of land are essential factors influencing investment decisions. In Belarus not only is available land scarce and difficult to access, but the procedures regulating its accessibility leave scope for the regional authorities to preclude the entry of foreign investors beyond the limits set by the Investment Code.

The new Land Code that came into force in January 2009 partially addressed these issues. The code sets the grounds for the development of a real estate market by making it possible to acquire title to land, easily transfer it and use it as collateral for bank credit. Until a sufficient number of titles are accessible through this market, however, investors will still need to obtain land title from the state (including office space), in what remains a highly bureaucratic and lengthy process.

The land regime is set by the Constitution, the Civil Code, the Code of the Republic of Belarus on Land and various decrees and edicts of the President and of the government.

Following the Constitution, the mineral wealth, waters, forests and all land for agricultural use are the sole and exclusive property of the state. These constitute more than 90 per cent of the country's territory.

Until recently, parcels within the remaining 9.3 per cent of non-agricultural land could be leased, allocated for life with right of inheritance or purchased, though only by individuals or Belarusian non-governmental legal entities and only for specific purposes. The Land Code adopted in 2008 enables legal entities to acquire ownership in non-agricultural land. However, for the time being, ownership remains rare, as it relies primarily on the auctioning of ownership title to developed land. Since most developed land is owned by state enterprises, land acquisition falls within the privatization process and requires the case-by-case approval of the President of the Republic.

Leasehold is the most common form of title to land for foreign and domestic companies alike. A lease title can be transferred (subleased, contributed to the participation in the capital of economic associations and societies) and used as collateral against a bank credit. It is granted for a period of up to 99 years (renewable) and can be acquired through auction, through an ad hoc presidential decree or by purchasing the building/facilities that are grounded on the land parcel.

According to the authorities, obtaining a title used to take up to four years until a recent reform (Presidential Edict 667 of 2007) helped speed up the process. But investors still need to go through a complicated procedure involving many different steps and government authorities. If the investor has already identified the land he/she would like to have access to, the following procedure applies:

1. The first step is to request a preliminary agreement from the Regional Executive Committee where the land is located, by presenting a request for lease based on a detailed investment proposal. The request should contain the planned location of the land, its functional purpose, the volume of the planned investment and guarantees regarding the source of the funds to invest. Within three days of receiving the request, the Regional Executive Committee can reject the request based on its inconsistency with the city plan or with environmental and other conditions prescribed by the law. A refusal can be appealed in court;

2. If accepted, the request is transferred to the Regional Land Planning Organization, which prepares the land cadastral documents (25 days to two months) and transfers them to a commission composed of representatives of the Regional Executive Committee, the Regional Land Planning, the geodesy service of State Property Committee, the Ministry of Environmental Protection, the Emergency Services, the Sanitary Control and the Architecture and Construction Authority. This commission has five days to confirm the suitability of the plot for the purpose indicated by the investor.[56] A contract is then issued between the Regional Land Planning Organization and the investor, based on which the organization will facilitate the remaining steps. The contract requirements should be completed within two months and require the investor to present, once more, a similar set of documents to those requested by the Regional Executive Authority for the pre-approval;[57]

3. The remaining steps are internal to the administration. They involve obtaining further review and authorization from the Organization of Land Planning (three days), the Local Authority of Architecture and Building (three days) and the Organization of Land Planning and Geodesy (five days);

4. Upon conclusion of the above process, the Regional Executive Committee organizes an auction on the identified plot (the starting price is based on an evaluation by a state property evaluator). Therefore, the investor who originally requested the land is not certain to obtain it unless she/he is the only bidder;

5. Finally, the investor is given six months to start construction or business activities on the assigned plot. Otherwise, the plot can be withdrawn by the Regional Authorities with court approval and without compensation.

Investors who have not pre-identified their investment location can directly participate in the regional authorities' auctions for available plots, which are made public on the Internet. Land can be acquired without an auction only to build construction projects in a FEZ or if a particular construction project and investor are prescribed by presidential decisions or by a State Development Programme. In these cases, the land is assigned by decree.

In this case, the functional usage of land plots is very strictly determined prior to auction. For instance, a typical auction would indicate that a plot is available for the establishment of a specific activity, such as a bank or a supermarket. The size of the facility to be built is also specified in advance. Interested investors

---

[56] The Chair of Regional Executive Committee should confirm the act.
[57] These include the confirmation of preliminary alignment, general building plan and state expertise, confirmation on the existence of investment funds, the copy of registration certificate and charter documents.

need to present the regional executive authorities with a business plan featuring the planned activities, scale etc., as in the scenario described above. Evaluation criteria also include matching the economic and social objectives of the city/region. This is vaguely defined and leaves room for arbitrary outcomes.

The procedure described above assumes that a land plot is available, properly zoned and suitable for the functional purpose indicated by the investor. These conditions, however, are seldom satisfied in Belarus. In the absence of a suitable plot of land following a positive review of the investor's investment plan, the regional authorities must apply to the central authorities for rezoning agricultural into industrial or commercial land. This is a slow and intricate procedure that requires the regional authorities to obtain the approval from the Ministry of Architecture, the State Property Fund and ultimately the Council of Ministers or the President. Following the decision of the central authorities, the plot is offered in an open auction and may either be rented or sold.

An alternative regime is that of the temporary (up to 10 years) or permanent (up to 99 years) use of existing state property, which is accessed through a request to the regional authorities. This regime provides faster access to title, but the scope of the right is more limited compared to leasehold, since the fruition title cannot be transferred or used as collateral in banks.

The authorities are aiming at speeding up the zoning and auctioning of land in the coming years, but as of May 2008, only around 170 plots were ready for auction. As a result, it has been often the case that large investors accessed the land directly by means of a dedicated presidential decree. As indicated, the new Land Code should eventually lead to the emergence of a private market for land, where it will be possible to transfer lease title among private entities by simply notifying the cadastral authorities.

In the meantime, however, it is recommended that access to land be facilitated in a number of ways:

- The state authorities should support each region in the identification and zoning of sufficient land areas to be allocated to commercial or industrial use, but freed from the tight functional purpose specifications of the current system. Pre-zoning and broader functional specification would significantly shorten the access procedure while retaining the current auctioning principle;
- In the context of the recommended regional competitiveness benchmarking (see section A), regions should be rated against each other with respect to the support offered to investors in facilitating land access. By this means, the central government would annually review their performance and intervene in support of those regions where land access is particularly problematic;
- In parallel, the government should continue to streamline both the procedures for land zoning and those for land allocation by carrying out a step-by-step analysis of the current administrative and procedural requirements with a view at eliminating superfluous steps and rationalizing the coordination between the local and central authorities.

8. Environment

As the single country most affected by the radioactive contamination resulting from the Chernobyl nuclear power station accident in 1986, Belarus has traditionally paid much attention to environmental protection.[58] The legal pillar of environmental protection is the Law on Protecting the Environment (of 1992, as amended in 2002), which is complemented by a series of governmental resolutions, decisions and presidential edicts and decrees. Together, they provide for a sound environmental impact assessment regime.

---

[58] According to the United Nations Economic Commission for Europe, 23 per cent of the country (more than 6,000 km2) remains contaminated by caesium-137 although a network of hundreds of laboratories belonging to different governmental agencies is adequately monitoring radionuclides in agricultural and other products.

In accordance with international good practice, activities with potentially adverse environmental impact must undergo different levels of permitting/screening, depending on their damage potential as described below.

Activities requiring an environmental licence. These include the geological exploration of the subsoil, water wells drilling, use, neutralization and burial of dangerous waste and other environmentally hazardous activities, as per Presidential Decree 17 of 2003 and Council of Ministers Resolution 1271 of 2003. Reportedly, once all necessary documentation is produced by the investors, the licensing procedure is speedy and efficient.

Activities requiring an environmental permit and a detailed environmental impact assessment. While licences are needed for specific types of activities, environmental permits are required for any activity that may generate pollution over certain limits envisaged in the Belarusian legislation.[59] Moreover, among these activities, those with the highest pollution potential must undergo an environmental impact assessment, based on an expert evaluation of the project. Such an assessment must not take longer than two months after all needed documents are submitted to the regulator.[60]

Activities requiring only an environmental permit as a part of their project documentation. These are the activities with low environmental impact risk, for which the permitting procedure is streamlined.

The Ministry of Natural Resources and Environmental Protection handles primarily large projects (including those above $5 million). For smaller projects, it delegates authority to representatives at local and regional level. The ministry reports satisfaction with the level of expertise and resources necessary to deal with the permitting, monitoring and control of the environmentally sensitive activities. The business community expressed concern over the severe sanctions imposed even in cases of minor violations of the environmental regulation.

9. Governance issues

The ease of complying with government regulations, the incidence of corruption, the effectiveness and predictability of the judiciary and the enforceability of contracts all affect investors' confidence in committing their capital and effort to a country. In Belarus, none of these issues constitutes an obstacle impossible for foreign investors to overcome. Nonetheless, a major effort on many of these counts is necessary to create a more favourable business environment. A comparison with its immediate neighbours is a case in point.

For example, giving one perspective, at the end of June 2008, the World Bank published its annual Governance Matters Report, which presents six aggregate governance indicators that are assembled using the data and methodology of 32 different international organizations. Table II.2 shows the results for Belarus and selected neighbouring countries for 2000 and 2007. As can be seen, Belarus scores high in terms of political stability and absence of violence. However, it was perceived to lag significantly behind in terms of regulatory quality and government effectiveness, respect for the rule of law, voice and accountability or control of corruption, in particular when compared to Latvia. Moreover, while between 2000 and 2007 Belarus only progressed with respect to political stability and regulatory quality, during the same period, its neighbours made progress in most areas of governance.

---

[59] With the exception of those activities falling within the list of sources of pollution for which no limits are applied, as determined by the Resolution of the Ministry of Natural Resources and Environmental Protection 10 of 2005.

[60] Ministry for Natural Resources and Environmental Protection, resolution 1 of 2001, article 13.

Table II.2. Governance indicators for Belarus, Latvia, the Russian Federation and Ukraine, 2000 and 2007

	Year	Belarus		Latvia		Russian Federation		Ukraine	
		% rank[1]	Est.[2]	% rank	Est.	% rank	Est.	% rank	Est.
Voice and accountability	2007	4	-1.80	74	0.86	20	-1.01	45	-0.09
	2000	11	-1.35	70	0.71	34	-0.46	31	-0.57
Political stability and absence of violence	2007	53	0.20	71	0.72	23	-0.75	50	0.16
	2000	40	-0.14	66	0.61	24	-0.69	34	-0.37
Government effectiveness	2007	9	-1.26	71	0.55	42	-0.40	30	-0.60
	2000	21	-0.81	70	0.49	33	-0.60	28	-0.65
Regulatory quality	2007	5	-1.56	84	1.06	35	-0.44	36	-0.42
	2000	3	-1.94	73	0.68	19	-0.78	26	-0.62
Rule of law	2007	12	-1.09	66	0.57	17	-0.97	28	-0.70
	2000	16	-1.04	59	0.22	16	-1.05	18	-0.97
Control of corruption	2007	19	-0.88	66	0.31	16	-0.92	27	-0.73
	2000	35	-0.57	58	0.04	12	-0.98	11	-1.01

Source: World Bank, Governance Matters 2008.
Notes: [1] Country's percentile rank, where 0 corresponds to the lowest rank and 100 to the highest rank.
[2] Estimate of governance measured on a scale from approximately -2.5 to 2.5. Higher values correspond to higher ranks in the governance index.

Ease of regulatory compliance and transparency issues

Notwithstanding the ongoing simplification effort, complying with business legislation in Belarus is still a challenge for both foreign and domestic investors. Entrepreneurship is subject to prolific legislative activity (the Administrative Code, for instance, has been revised more than 25 times since its adoption in 2003) that imposes on all companies, including SMEs, a large number of administrative requirements. These translate into additional costs for business, thus reducing the competitiveness of Belarus as an investment location.

As already mentioned, one of the most difficult problems is dealing with licensing and permit requirements. The administrative bodies themselves calculated that more than 1,000 permits exist for entrepreneurs at the national and local levels.[61] All companies in Belarus are also subject to extensive and resource-intensive reporting requirements from a range of government agencies. Most forms are paper-based only and need to be filed monthly with local and state departments. Reporting is not only for statistical purposes. For instance, according to investors interviewed by UNCTAD, companies need to fill in a form for the purchase of each tire of a car. Reporting requirements are also connected to price control mechanisms, though these apply exclusively to Belarusian investors (see chapter III).

Entrepreneurial activity in Belarus is also subject to a very high number of administrative controls. The International Financial Corporation (IFC) has prepared a report on Control and Supervision Activities in Belarus (2008),[62] based on interviews with 525 heads and owners of SMEs and individual entrepreneurs, from all sectors of the economy. According to the study, the annual average number of inspections to an average company has decreased from 10 in 2004 to four in 2006, and their duration from 24 to six days.[63] However, the study concludes that many of the remaining inspections are hardly justified and often unrelated to the

---

[61] IPM Research Centre (2007b).
[62] http://www.ifc.org/ifcext/belarus.nsf/AttachmentsByTitle/IFCBelarusSurvey2007_RU.pdf/$FILE/IFCBelarusSurvey2007_RU.pdf
[63] According to the IPM Research Centre, the number of inspections is higher, amounting to 7 to 8 inspections per SME in the first nine months of 2006 alone (IPM, 2007a).

risks or hazards posed by the inspected company.[64] The complexity and obscurity of the inspection norms and procedures make it difficult for companies to be aware of and understand them. This results in a high violation rate and high penalties, leading the IFC to conclude that inspections in Belarus have a fiscal rather than a preventive character. In this regard, Presidential Decree 689 of 2008 goes in the welcome direction of reducing the types of controls on the activities of legal entities and individual entrepreneurs.

The excessive regulation of entrepreneurial activity reduces the competitiveness of the local productive sector vis-à-vis Belarus' regional competitors and fosters the development of the informal (shadow) economy. In addition, the countless administrative procedures and business regulations create a nourishing environment for rent-seeking behaviour. Transparency indicators show that corruption is a growing problem for the Belarusian administrative system, as shown in table II.3.

Table II.3.   Corruption perception index, Belarus and comparative countries, 2001–2007

Economy	2001	2002	2003	2004	2005	2006	2007
Belarus	n/a	36	53	74	107	151	150
Lithuania	38	36	41	44	44	46	51
Poland	44	45	64	67	70	61	61
Russian Federation	79	71	86	90	126	121	143
Ukraine	83	85	106	122	107	99	118

Source: Transparency International.

The key legal instruments for the fight against corruption are already present in the Belarusian legislation. For instance, the Criminal Code (Law 275-3 of 1999) clearly defines corruption, abuse of power and accepting or taking bribes as crimes that can lead to imprisonment. Moreover, Belarus signed and ratified the United Nations Convention against Corruption in 1995. More recently, the authorities have introduced a series of new initiatives, including a special Law on the Fight against Corruption (Law 122 of 2006) and a new State Programme on the Fight against Corruption for 2007–2010 (Presidential Edict 220 of 2007). Both are meant to promote effective anti-corruption activities and adopt a preventive approach. However, the most effective tool in the fight against corruption, in the case of Belarus, might be to continue the legislative simplification and to review the transparency of the existing laws. In this regard, encouraging recent initiatives aimed at reducing state regulation and state control of economic activities have been adopted. These include the introduction of the declaratory principle in the state registration process and a reduction in the registration paperwork, as well as the narrowing of the bases for forced liquidation of economic entities and for the curtailment of the activities of individual entrepreneurs (Presidential Decree 1 of 2009).

Nonetheless, it should remain a high priority to continue the work of the special working group led by the Deputy Prime Minister established in late 2006 to propose simplifications of the administrative procedures.

Enforcement of contracts

One area of particular concern to foreign investors is that of the time and cost necessary to enforce contracts. Belarus has a court system consisting of the Constitutional Court, courts of general jurisdiction with the Supreme Court at the head and economic courts with the Supreme Economic Court at the head. Foreign investors interviewed by UNCTAD during the course of this review expressed satisfaction with the functioning of the economic courts, which are considered speedy and unbiased. The efficiency of the

---

[64]   For example, in 2006, around 64 per cent of SMEs hosted inspections by the fire safety agency, although the majority of them are not related to sectors or industries with a high fire risk. Likewise, 42 per cent of SMEs were inspected by the sanitary agencies, when only 12 per cent of all them were related to production of food, medicine, children's goods, etc. (IPM, 2008).

Belarusian economic courts is confirmed by the international rankings on contract enforcement published by the Doing Business Report of the World Bank, which show that Belarus ranks fourteenth in the world for the effectiveness of its courts in enforcing contracts, above all the neighbouring countries in the sample of table II.4.

Table II.4   Contract enforcement, Belarus and comparative countries, 2008

Economy	Enforcing Contracts			
	Rank	Procedures (number)	Time (days)	Cost (% of debt)
Belarus	14	28	225	23.4
Lithuania	16	30	210	23.6
Poland	68	38	830	12
Russian Federation	18	37	281	13.4
Ukraine	49	30	354	41.5

Source: World Bank, Doing Business Database.

10. Protection of intellectual property

The system of intellectual property protection and administration in Belarus is relatively young. However, in the few years since its establishment, Belarus has been striving to put in place the legal conditions for effective intellectual property protection and commercialization.

The Constitution of the Republic of Belarus guarantees freedom of artistic, scientific, technical creativity and protection of the rights of inventors, intellectual property creators and right owners. The intellectual potential of the nation is acknowledged as a determinant factor in the socio-economic development of the country.

Belarus is party to 17 international treaties administered by the World Intellectual Property Organization (WIPO). These include, among others, the Paris Convention (industrial property), the Patent Cooperation Treaty, the Berne Convention (copyright), the WIPO Copyright Treaty, the Rome Convention (related rights), the WIPO Performances and Phonograms Treaty and the Madrid Agreement (international registration of marks).

The national legislation on intellectual property includes normative and legal acts elaborated in cooperation with WIPO and takes into account international standards in this sphere, including TRIPS (Trade-Related Aspects of Intellectual Property Rights) requirements. It comprises the Civil Code of Belarus, which identifies the objects of intellectual property rights (article 980), but also special laws including the Law on Copyright and Related Rights (as amended, 1998); the Law on Patents for Inventions, Utility Models and Industrial Designs (as amended, 2004); the Law on Trademarks and Service Marks (as amended in 2000 and 2006); the Law on Geographical Identification (as amended, 2004); the Law on Patents on Plant Varieties (as amended, 2004); and the Law on the Legal Protection of Integrated Circuit Topography (as amended, 2004). Finally, the Criminal Code and the Code on Administrative Violations provide for criminal and administrative penalties to be applied in cases of infringement of patents, copyright and related rights.

Implementation of government policy in the field of intellectual property is the responsibility of the State Committee on Science and Technology. Subordinated to the committee, the National Intellectual Property Centre (NIPC) functions as the national intellectual property office in charge of registering patent and licence agreements, concession agreements and other agreements in the area of intellectual property.[65]

---

[65] Technology transfer contracts are not subjected to screening and the only requirement is to register the licence agreements.

The NIPC Appeal Board is also involved in the pre-court settlement of any intellectual property-related disputes, while judiciary settlement is carried out by the Judicial Board for Intellectual Property Issues of the Supreme Court. The State Commission on Intellectual Property Rights Protection and Intellectual Property Violation Control under the Council of Ministers is the coordination body that ensures the cooperation of all ministries and other state agencies in the area of intellectual property protection and enforcement.

Material authors' rights with respect to works of science, literature and art are granted for the lifetime of the author and 50 years following the author's death. Invention patents are valid for 20 years with a possible five-year extension. Trademarks are granted for 10 years with the possibility of repeated extensions of 10 years each. Renewable utility models are granted for five years with a possible extension for three more years, while industrial design patents are granted for 10 years with a possible extension of five years. If the patent holder so requires, violation of the exclusive rights is to be desisted and the violator is obliged to compensate the patent holder for the losses incurred according to the legislation.

According to the authorities, the key remaining challenge with respect to the protection of intellectual property rights in Belarus is to raise awareness of the importance of intellectual property protection and commercialization within the country, as the majority of Belarusian managers and business representatives have little knowledge of commercial intellectual property use. To address the issue, an intellectual property training centre was set up within NIPC with the assistance of WIPO in 2004. The centre has provided training to more than 7,000 specialists so far. In this respect, it may prove useful to have commercial judges trained on various intellectual property issues as well.

Finally, the key intellectual property legislation is currently under review. The objective is to ensure harmonization with Russian legislation and full compliance with the WTO intellectual property-related provisions in view of Belarus' planned accession to the WTO.

11. Competition policy

Belarus first adopted a basic legal framework to protect its economy and consumers against anti-competitive behaviour in 1992. However, the institutional framework for the protection of competition and the enforcement of pro-competitive measures remain inadequate. In an economic context where production is largely in the hands of SOEs, the development of the private sector requires abandoning discriminatory practices in the access to production inputs, in pricing policy or in the allocation of state subsidies. It cannot be assumed that reducing administrative and regulatory barriers to private investment will lead, in itself, to a reduction in the anti-competitive behaviour of established firms. Nor it can be assumed that the entry of TNCs will necessarily create more market contestability. Pro-competition measures need to be put in place. Addressing these issues should receive the highest priority.

The Law on Counteraction to Monopolistic Activities and Promotion of Competition of 1992 (last amended in January 2008) establishes the organizational and legal framework to prevent and suppress monopolistic activity. The law assigns a number of typical anti-trust functions to the state anti-monopoly body, but specifies that several other entities may act as anti-monopoly bodies. This role is currently performed by the Department on Price Policy of the Ministry of Economy, i.e. the same ministry that is responsible for SOEs, together with the Administrations on Price Policy of the Regional Economic Committees. The delimitation of powers and competence within this institutional setting is generally based on territorial factors (i.e., whether the anti-competitive behaviour has region- or state-wide effects). However, cases involving foreigners and cases of strategic importance to the state are the exclusive jurisdiction of the ministry.[66] The approval of both the ministry and the regional offices is necessary in the case of the reorganization of economic entities, their association or share transactions in which a foreign legal or physical person participates.

---

[66] See Resolution of the Ministry of Economy 57 of 2006 on the Approval of Agreements Hindering Competition.

According to the legislation, forbidden monopolistic activities include agreements and actions of companies obstructing competition and the abuse of dominant position. Importantly, agreements involving the state or state economic entities that may result in limitation of competition are also prohibited. The granting of tax reliefs and other privileges to certain companies on a discriminatory basis is possible, but subject to the approval of the anti-monopoly body.

Such discrimination is more evident in the access to raw materials and inputs, which favours SOEs over private companies, domestic and foreign alike. It also manifests itself in the allocation of government subsidies or in the access to finance. Anti-competitive effects are further produced by the application of price control regulations. The authorities control prices by directly setting their level (such as for "socially important" products), fixing maximum price increase indexes (such as the monthly price increase cap of 0.5 per cent above which any company must receive approval by the authorities[67]) or establishing the methods of price settings. Enterprises are also obliged to provide economic justification of prices and calculations in special forms provided by law.[68] Importantly, companies with foreign participation are excluded from the price control legislation. This risks creating strong distortions in the internal market and puts local enterprises at a competitive disadvantage (see more in chapter III of this report).

Dominant position is defined in the law as "the exclusive position of an economic entity or several economic entities on a market of commodity having no substitutes, or substitutional commodities, allowing it an opportunity to influence the general conditions of commodity circulation on a certain market, or hamper access to the commodity market for other economic entities" (article 1). The law leaves it to each competent authority to set the minimum thresholds for determining dominant position and to define the relevant market criteria. The Department of Pricing Policies at the Ministry of Economy maintains a "state registry on economic subjects having dominant position in the Belarusian market for goods". As at August 2008, there were 153 companies in the list, down from 181 in 2006.

Abuse of dominant position may be considered lawful when the company proves that its activity was carried out in execution of the legislative acts of the Republic. This counters international practice, according to which exceptions to anti-monopolistic behaviour are judged based on their positive effects on consumers. Moreover, according to investors, business regulators are in a position to offer to selected businesses conditions of reduced competition or even no competition, by means of customized regulatory application.[69]

State, natural and extreme (i.e. temporary and authorized by the state) monopolies are also lawful and regulated by law.

Violation of the antitrust legislation can result in the imposition of administrative fines and indemnification payments.

No reference to mergers and acquisitions (M&A) is contained in the law. Nevertheless, the law refers to the concept of "reorganization of a legal entity", which sets a number of criteria and principles regulating M&A activity (article 12). For instance, prior approval of the anti-competition body is required for the acquisition of shares or other assets of one entity by another if the latter already has a 30 per cent market share (lowered to 25 per cent if it confers decisive influence on an entity with dominant position). However no threshold has been set for mergers to date, although it figures in a draft presidential decree aimed at strengthening anti-monopolistic legislation.

---

[67] Resolution of the Council of Minister 944 of 1999, Regulation of the Council of Ministers of December 30, 2006 on Some Measures on Securing the Predictive Inflation Indicator in 2007, reconfirmed in the letter of the Ministry of Economy 481 of March 2008 on the Limit of Price Increase.

[68] GET (2007).

[69] See World Bank (2005).

Adoption of the draft decree would be a welcome step, as the competition policy and regime in Belarus need significant strengthening. The size and significance of SOEs (chapter I) associated with existing discriminatory practices are among the most important issues Belarus needs to address in the short and medium term. The policy and attitude that the government will adopt as SOEs and emerging Belarusian private enterprises come under increasing competitive pressure from FDI will be key determinants of the investment climate in the near future. A significant number of SOEs are likely to face bankruptcy when confronted with hard budget constraints (i.e. when they are cut off from state subsidies and no longer have access to loans from state-owned commercial terms on special terms) and competition from the private sector. This review stresses that a properly level playing field will be key to maximizing the benefits of FDI for the development of the local private sector and reducing potential crowding out effects (chapter III).

It is thus recommended to:

- Review all discriminatory practices with respect to the access to inputs with a view to removing distortions where these are not strictly justified by public interest;
- Remove price limitations for all but a relatively narrowly defined list of public goods;
- Create an independent, professionally staffed and adequately funded National Competition Authority;
- Expand the competition law so as to include:
  - A precise definition of abuse of dominant position, including the minimum market share threshold and the conditions for exceptions to be lawful;
  - The control of M&A;
- Introduce working mechanisms for coordination between the National Competition Authority, the competent regional authorities and other regulatory bodies on the different proceedings.

In this context, it could be helpful for Belarus to review its competition regime against UNCTAD's model competition law.

12. Assessment

The main aim of this chapter was to review the legal framework in Belarus and evaluate the extent to which it is conducive to the attraction of foreign investors and their operations in the country. This review of general measures in the investment framework has four key general findings:

1. Although the investment code contains only a few restrictions to FDI, investment policy and regulations continue to reflect a "steer and control" approach. The authorities see their role as one of steering private investments where they see the most need, as illustrated in the preparation of comprehensive "lists of projects calling for investment" by most ministries and regions;

2. The reform process started in late 2007 has improved the regulatory framework for the operations of foreign investors in Belarus. The main examples can be found in the areas of land, taxation, state registration and licensing, and the entry of foreign labour. However, it fell short of bringing the legislation up to international good standards. Entrepreneurial activity continues to be the object of excessive regulation, reporting requirements and administrative controls that increase the cost of doing business and lead to transparency and governance issues;

3. The effectiveness of the recent reforms, which stem from the top levels of the administration, often meets the resistance of the administrative machinery, held back by inadequacies in the coordination between the central and regional levels of the state or by the existence of local regulatory bottlenecks. This is the case particularly in the areas of permitting, licensing, land and taxation;

4. While in many areas of the regulatory framework, such as environmental permits, the enforcement of contracts and the intellectual property protection regime are functional, key gaps and bottlenecks persist. These relate particularly to the inadequacy of the competition regime and rigidities in the price and wage determination process.

CHAPTER III

THE ROLE OF FDI FOR SME DEVELOPMENT

The overall development objective of the Belarusian Government is to improve the standard of living of its population by effectively fostering and utilizing human capital, upgrading technology, encouraging structural changes and ultimately raising competitiveness. The aims and basic principles of this objective are stated in the Programme of Social and Economic Development of the Republic of Belarus for 2006–2010. Innovation is a major element of the development of the productive sectors under this programme.[70] In this regard, the policy recognizes the positive direct effect of SMEs on social and economic development and the need for an integrated system of reforms, including policies and measures related to taxation, credit, finance, prices, competition and infrastructure.

In the context of this programme, the government has set ambitious objectives and targets for the development of the SME sector by 2010. These comprise creating an enabling environment conducive to SME development, intensifying investment and innovation activities in the SME sector and stimulating entrepreneurship. Targets associated with the programme also include increasing the SME share of total sales and total employment in the economy.

Against this background, the government has requested UNCTAD to elaborate a strategy to utilize FDI to foster the development of the Belarusian SME sector. In this regard, the explicit commitments of the government to attract FDI and develop the SME sector become central elements of an FDI strategy that would support the achievement of these objectives. The proposed strategy stems from a review of both the economic issues and the practical experience regarding the conditions and policies that make FDI work for the development of local SMEs (section A); an analysis of the specificities of the Belarusian SME sector (section B); and a description of the current policy and institutional support infrastructure for SMEs (section C). As a result, it recommends a comprehensive set of measures aimed at supporting the development of local productive capacities through FDI (section D).

The key element of the strategy is the removal of existing obstacles to private sector development, in particular those affecting the daily operation of SMEs, including price and administrative controls, unfair competition with SOEs and a heavy regulatory and administrative burden. The effectiveness of specific supporting measures and policies is and will remain limited until these issues are tackled and SMEs are in conditions to compete and access local and international value chains. The complementary elements of the proposed strategy aim at enabling Belarus to effectively target the type of FDI that would most contribute to its objectives and to better utilize the channels for the transmission of the gains from FDI by promoting the absorptive capacities of its SMEs and designing a comprehensive supplier linkages programme.

A. Maximizing the benefits and minimizing the costs of FDI

A country's ability to attract FDI depends on many factors, including its initial economic conditions and policy environment. Beyond attracting FDI, it is important to identify ways in which its benefits can be maximized and its costs minimized. FDI can represent a significant source of private capital inflows for transition economies and can generate new production capacity and employment. In particular, FDI may bring new management techniques, technology, skills and access to larger markets. Furthermore, if well integrated into the local economy it can also generate additional positive effects, including chiefly through linkages. However, FDI may also generate costs (e.g. by poaching skilled workers from local firms, making access to credit more difficult where TNC borrowers may be favoured over local firms and crowding out local firms through increased competition). The magnitude of positive and negative effects is a function of

---

[70] http://www.president.gov.by/en/press23869.html

several factors, including the country's context and the composition of FDI. In many cases where net benefits are low – or where costs exceed benefits – it is generally due to shortcomings in the policy environment (Organization for Economic Cooperation and Development (OECD), 2002).

Based on a review of the main economic issues and the international experience on the potential effects of FDI (positive and negative) on a host country's SME sector, the following sections describe the optimal conditions and the policies that help maximize the benefits and reduce the costs of FDI. An enabling environment for business (e.g. an adequate regulatory framework) and a sufficiently developed domestic capacity are crucial to attract FDI and ensure that the host country economy can take full advantage of FDI.

1. Spillover effects

TNCs typically operate along global supply chains and source inputs from internationally competitive suppliers. Global supply chains of TNCs often extend across several countries and regions with TNCs focusing on core competencies and outsourcing operations where they do not have a competitive advantage, thus reducing costs and increasing profitability. TNCs frequently partner with local firms including SMEs, building complex supplier networks of competitive local enterprises, depending on several factors including cost, availability of inputs and market conditions (UNCTAD, 2006a).

In many countries, a major motivation for attracting FDI is to promote increases in the overall productivity and competitiveness of the economy. By offering new supply chains to enterprises, TNCs can provide a market test for local products (i.e. allowing local products to be benchmarked internationally) and add competitiveness to existing competence. Such gains may translate into broader benefits and enhanced competitiveness for the economy as a whole through productivity spillovers, contributing to industrial transformation and upgrading of value added activities, improved export performance, higher national income and better employment opportunities. In this case, positive productivity spillovers or externalities are benefits to the host economy beyond those captured directly by the TNC. The presence of TNCs may improve the productivity of local firms through productivity spillovers due to knowledge and technology transfer (i.e. human capital spillovers and demonstration effects) and competition effects. There is significant evidence to suggest that the productivity of domestic firms is positively correlated with the presence of TNCs through productivity spillovers (Javorick and Spatareanu, 2005).

Spillovers may be horizontal (intra-industry) or vertical (inter-industry). Vertical spillovers may occur as a result of linkages between buyers and suppliers (box III.1) and be forward (downstream industries) or backward (upstream industries). Horizontal productivity spillovers may occur where a local firm increases its productivity by copying technologies or marketing techniques of a TNC (through demonstration effects or by hiring workers trained by the TNC). In the Czech Republic and Latvia, survey evidence from the manufacturing sector shows that domestic firms reported learning about new technologies and marketing techniques from TNCs within the same industry, as well as benefiting from the knowledge of workers previously employed by TNCs (Javorick, forthcoming).

Box III.1. Types of linkages

Backward linkages with suppliers: when a TNC obtains goods and/or services (e.g. parts, components, other inputs) from a domestic firm. These may range from transactions to close inter-firm cooperation.

Forward linkages with buyers: are present when TNCs outsource the distribution of their goods and/or services to domestic firms or when TNCs provide extensive after-sales services.

Horizontal linkages: represent linkages with competing domestic firms.

Source: UNCTAD (forthcoming a).

However, some studies show that technology spillovers are more likely between TNCs and local suppliers (inter-industry) than with local competitors (intra-industry). Where firms compete in the same industry, the TNC may have the incentive to prevent technology leakage and spillovers, for example through formal protection of their intellectual property (Javorick, 2004). In contrast, TNCs may have the incentive to promote technology transfer to suppliers through vertical linkages as they are likely to benefit from the improved performance of suppliers (for example, through lower costs and higher quality inputs).

Some domestic firms may be affected adversely if competition with multinationals (intra-industry) reduces their market share leading to lower production levels and hence decreased productivity in the short run. Alternatively, they may fail to benefit from the presence of FDI where TNCs source inputs internationally rather than in the local market (inter-industry). Domestic industries and enterprises that find it difficult to produce in a more competitive environment may be crowded out, potentially hindering endogenous technological development. Nevertheless, costs to certain local firms may lead to more efficient outcomes for the overall economy. Also, increased competition may force local firms to raise their efficiency and/or search for new technology in order to remain competitive (competition effects) in the long run (Blomström and Kokko, 1998). Survey evidence from the Czech Republic and Latvia shows a small but significant percentage of respondents (29 per cent) reporting a loss in market share to TNCs (Javorick, forthcoming).

The literature finds more evidence of vertical spillovers, particularly through backward linkages, with some of the findings showing little or no evidence of horizontal spillovers (Javorick and Spatareanu, 2005; Djankov and Hoekman, 2000; Konings, 2001). There are different channels through which vertical spillovers may occur (Javorick, 2004; Javorick and Spatareanu, 2005).[71]

- Local suppliers may benefit from direct assistance and knowledge transfer from TNCs;
- Increased demand from TNCs for inputs from local suppliers can typically allow firms to increase productivity through economies of scale;
- Local firms may improve their performance while supplying TNCs as a result of higher requirements (e.g. quality, on-time delivery, quantity), transfer of knowledge and greater competition. In particular, local firms can face competition from foreign suppliers as well as local ones when supplying TNCs. Also, local firms who want to continue supplying the TNC will have the incentive to improve performance.

2. Optimal conditions and policies for positive spillover effects

Positive spillovers from TNCs may be significant; however, they are neither automatic nor guaranteed. They vary depending on the characteristics of the host country, including the policy environment and the industry (Blomström and Kokko, 1998). There are a number of factors that influence the extent to which the host country and domestic firms may benefit from FDI spillover effects. Many of these channels are interdependent and therefore should not be considered in isolation (Blomström et al., 2000). These include:

- **Absorptive capacity and technology gap**: the ability of local firms to absorb and utilize the technology spillovers from TNCs depends on several factors including the availability of skilled labour and levels of research and development spending. Local absorptive capacity is necessary to ensure that FDI fosters improvements in quality and competitiveness of the local supply base. Where absorptive capacity is lacking, domestic firms may find it difficult to compete and therefore are likely to be crowded out of the market. Empirical evidence suggests that absorptive capacity is the most important determinant of the ability of domestic firms to capture spillover effects from FDI (Crespo and Fontoura, 2007; Blomström et al., 2000). Evidence from the Czech manufacturing sector suggests that domestic firms benefit from technological spillovers from TNCs when they have the capacity to absorb technology through research and development spending (Kinoshita, 2001). The larger the technology gap between foreign and domestic firms, the less likely it is that host country firms have

---

[71] Vertical spillovers may not occur where TNCs contract firms that are already capable of producing inputs to the necessary standards.

the human capital and technological know-how to benefit from the technology transferred by the multinationals and, hence, the lower the potential for positive spillovers. In fact, spillovers may not occur where the technology gap is too large (Blomström and Sjöholm, 1999). Nevertheless, some level of technology gap is necessary for useful technology transfer to occur. Government policies encouraging research and development may help improve the ability of host country firms to absorb foreign technology. Direct measures that require technology transfer commitments from TNCs will enhance potential spillovers but may also discourage FDI (through, for instance, reduced profitability of FDI) and ultimately technology transfer;

- **Technology-sourcing versus technology-exploiting**: when locating abroad, TNCs may bring some level of technology in order to compete with local firms that have a better knowledge of the domestic markets (technology-exploiting). TNCs may also locate in a given country to gain access to technology (technology-sourcing). Naturally, spillovers are more likely to occur when FDI is technology-exploiting. Targeting the right investors is a professional exercise in which many investment promotion agencies worldwide engage significant resources;

- **Education and labour policies**: education policies and measures, including measures to improve labour skills through training, have an important influence on the absorptive capacity and human capital spillovers arising from the movement of labour. Also, reducing restrictions on labour mobility and promoting labour mobility will encourage human capital spillovers;

- **Competition**: increased competitiveness generally encourages TNCs to introduce new technology more rapidly and more extensively to compete more effectively. This may stimulate faster technological adoption by local firms and encourage greater efficiency at the firm and industry level and ultimately increase economy-wide productivity;

- **Trade orientation**: liberal trade policies facilitate the importation of technology embodied in imported inputs and have the potential to encourage substantial technology transfer through stimulating increased competition. They tend to attract higher levels of FDI than inward-oriented regimes as a result of fewer market distortions and a larger potential market. Nevertheless, TNCs located in inward-oriented economies are likely to use technologies unavailable in the local economy therefore creating the potential for significant demonstration effects (Kokko et al., 2001);

- **Market orientation**: TNCs oriented to the domestic market may purchase more inputs locally than their export-oriented TNCs therefore increasing the possibility of spillovers (Altenburg, 2000). However, export-oriented TNCs are more likely to impose higher requirements and therefore necessitate larger productivity improvements by local suppliers and tend to have more advanced technologies, creating more opportunity for technology spillover;

- **Vertical linkages**: the closer the linkages between TNCs and local suppliers/buyers, the greater the possibility of technology and knowledge transfer to suppliers/buyers including the movement of labour between TNCs and domestic firms. Closer vertical linkages are associated with larger productivity spillovers to host country firms. Factors promoting closer vertical linkages include the technical capacity of local firms, the size of the host country market, use of inputs and local content requirements;

- **Domestic firm characteristics**: for instance, firms that produce for the domestic market may be more likely to benefit from spillover effects given that domestic exporting firms already face substantial competition and therefore TNCs are unlikely to increase competitiveness pressures (Crespo and Fontoura, 2007; Blomström and Sjöholm, 1999). In contrast, export-oriented domestic firms already exposed to international competition tend to be better at absorbing technology and maintaining competitiveness (Crespo and Fontoura, 2007). The size of firms may have an impact on the extent to which spillover effects materialize. Smaller firms may find it difficult to compete with TNCs and/or to produce at the necessary scale to utilize the available technologies;

• **FDI characteristics**: there are several characteristics of FDI that may influence spillovers to domestic firms (Crespo and Fontoura, 2007). For instance, the origin of FDI and associated differences in terms of culture, language, distance and modes of technology transfer are likely to affect the extent of spillovers. For example, the distance between the TNCs' home country and host country may have implications on the location of inputs sourcing due to transportation costs, differences in cultures and languages that may limit the domestic firms' ability to absorb new technology and membership in preferential trading arrangements that may influence sourcing patterns. Also, the way in which FDI takes place (greenfield versus M&A) may influence the degree of spillovers. For instance, technological introduction may be slower with mergers and acquisitions compared to greenfield investments where the introduction of new technology is immediate.

The government will need to identify the different levers, including supporting policies and measures, which encourage FDI and generate positive spillovers. Supporting policies and measures are necessary to maximize the benefits of FDI and mitigate the risks. The government should assess the effectiveness of supporting policies and measures in generating maximum spillover benefits and prioritize and sequence their implementation. For instance, government support to education and competiveness may be more effective than direct controls to secure technology transfer from TNCs to local firms (Kokko and Blomström, 1995). Given the interdependence of many of the factors and supporting policies and measures that determine FDI and associated spillovers, it is important that a set of mutually reinforcing policies and measures are developed and implemented (section D).

The following sections present the current status of the SME sector in Belarus (section B), as well as the policies and institutions that aim at fostering the sector's development and influence the extent of linkages between TNCs and SMEs and other potential spillover effects (section C).

B. The SME sector in Belarus

1. The Belarusian definition of small and medium enterprises

Although the term medium-sized enterprise is frequently used in official documents, the Belarusian Government, like the Russian Federation, has not adopted an official legislative or statistical definition of "medium-sized enterprises". It relies instead on the concept of small enterprises, which include enterprises employing up to a specific number of employees, according to the sector of activity (as per table III.1). As in other CIS countries, no financial criteria such as turnover or balance sheet enters the definition.

Table III.1.   Definition of small enterprises in Belarus

Branch of activity	Number of employees
Industry and transport	≤ 100
Agriculture	≤ 60
Construction and wholesale trade	≤ 50
Retail trade and personal services	≤ 30
Other non-productive branches	≤ 25

Source: Decree 262 of 1996 and Law on State Small Business Support of 16 October 1996.

Different countries define SMEs differently, which makes it difficult to establish an international comparison. However, further to the introduction by the European Commission, together with the European Investment Bank and the European Investment Fund, of a common definition of SMEs in 2003, a new international standard is emerging. This introduces a distinction between micro, small and medium-sized enterprises (table III.2). The objective is not only to ensure that supporting policy measures for the sector are applied consistently, but also to target such initiatives to relevant types of enterprises.

Table III.2.   Definition of SMEs in the European Union

Enterprise category	Number of staff	Turnover	or	Balance sheet total
Medium-sized	< 250	≤ €50 million		≤ €43 million
Small	< 50	≤ €10 million		≤ €10 million
Micro	< 10	≤ €2 million		≤ €2 million

Source: European Commission Recommendation 2003/361/EC as of 6 May 2003.

Having a standard SME definition makes the gathering and analyzing of statistical information about businesses easier. In this regard, it is advisable that Belarus adjusts its national definition to better match the emerging international standard. In addition to making international comparisons possible, therefore allowing more accurate benchmarking of performance, the international definition may encourage the adoption of measures addressing the specific problems of micro enterprises, especially during their start-up phase. For the purposes of the analysis of this chapter, however, the official definition of small enterprises adopted by Belarus will be used as a proxy for the entire SME sector.

2.   Statistical and comparative analysis

SMEs play a fundamental role in economic development and in most developed countries they often contribute more than 50 per cent of GDP. They typically generate much employment in developed, developing and transition economies, frequently accounting for 60 per cent or more of total employment. As described in the following section, although the number of SMEs in Belarus is growing rapidly, the sector is still at an incipient stage of development with a very limited contribution to the overall economy.

In 2007, the total number of small enterprises in Belarus had increased by 13,580 units compared to 2006, to reach 51,240 (an increase of 36 per cent).[72] The large majority of SMEs are private entities (94.1 per cent), while only 2.6 per cent are state-owned and 3.3 per cent foreign-owned.[73] The sector is characterized by low levels of development of formal growth-oriented medium-sized enterprises – the so-called "missing middle". Small and micro enterprises typically supply relatively small local markets, adopt basic and informal technologies and often have low levels of aggregate productivity (UNCTAD, 2006b).

There are over 200,000 individual entrepreneurs in Belarus. Most are informal and operate as retailers and street vendors. Among their main activities is the trade of goods through the open boundary with the Russian Federation. At the end of 2006, the President issued Edict 760 ordering that the majority of self-employed individual entrepreneurs register or reregister their businesses by converting them into unitary private enterprises (micro enterprises or any other legal corporate entity).[74] The objective is to facilitate the transition of individual entrepreneurs to unitary enterprises and to secure the formalization of such activities. Many entrepreneurs, however, are unwilling to reregister into unitary private enterprises due not only to possible higher taxes, but also to concerns regarding serious penalties that may be applied to them during the controls and inspections that affect formal businesses (see section D).

Although the number of SMEs is increasing rapidly, their contribution to total output of goods and services in Belarus is still extremely low, representing only about 8.2 per cent of GDP in 2007.[75] Table III.3 shows that the share of the SME sector in GDP is lower in Belarus than in any other CIS country or transition economy, reflecting the low level of participation of the private sector in the economy. Comparative employment figures also indicate that the contribution of small enterprises to total employment is lower in Belarus than in any other country in the region (with the exception of Ukraine), representing only 17 per cent of total employment.

---

[72] 1 January 2008, Ministry of Statistics and Analysis, Belarus.

[73] http://w3.economy.gov.by/ministry/economy.nsf/c0f0523c581097c9c225701900349321/96e90b88da41a2ffc225749b00486d6f?OpenDocument

[74] Edict of the President 760 of 31 December 2006 on Some Measures on the Regulation of Entrepreneurial Activity.

[75] According to preliminary estimates by the Ministry of Statistics and Analysis, this figure has grown to 8.4 per cent in the first quarter of 2008.

Table III.3.   Indicators of SME development, Belarus and other transition economies, 2007

Country	Share of private sector in GDP (per cent)	Share of SME sector in GDP (per cent)	Share of SME employees in total employment (per cent)
Albania	75	64	60
Armenia	75	40	35
Azerbaijan	60	26	53
Belarus	**25**	**8**	**17**
Bulgaria	75	39	51
Georgia	70	12	27
Republic of Moldova	65	27	22
Romania	70	55	57
Russian Federation	65	45	40
Serbia	55	65	56
Ukraine	65	10	15

Source: ERENET Database, 2007 and 2008, EBRD, Ministry of Economy and Ministry of Statistics and Analysis of Belarus.

A breakdown by activity of the total number of small enterprises (table III.4) shows that the relative majority are active in trade and catering (39.1 per cent), although the largest contributor to total output and employment within the sector are small enterprises involved in industrial activities (39.2 per cent and 38.5 per cent respectively). Construction is also an important area of activity for SMEs, both in terms of output (15.1 per cent) and employment (14.3 per cent).

Table III.4.   Small enterprises in Belarus, employment and output by activity, 2006

	Number of small enterprises		Average number of employees		Output of goods and services	
	total	% of total	total, persons	% of total	total, million (BYR)	% of total
Industry	8'409	22.3	162'997	38.5	5'384'133	39.2
Agriculture	2'312	6.1	10'256	2.4	234'184	1.7
Construction	4'400	11.7	63'952	15.1	1'952'801	14.3
Transport	1'930	5.1	32'179	7.6	912'022	6.7
Communication	172	0.5	1675	0.4	65'417	0.5
Trade and catering	14'716	39.1	109'420	25.8	2'842'507	20.8
Material supply and sales	394	1	3'270	0.8	77'276	0.6
Information and computer services	192	0.5	1'367	0.3	28'161	0.2
Real estate	1'040	2.8	6'393	1.5	145'314	1.1
General commercial activities	1'031	2.7	6'871	1.6	1'140'941	8.4
Other material production	338	0.9	2'606	0.6	85'219	0.6
Housing and communal services	95	0.3	826	0.2	14'449	0.1
Non-productive personal services	594	1.6	6'654	1.6	49'642	0.4
Health care and related	747	2	5'116	1.2	75'222	0.6
Education	135	0.4	1'241	0.3	19'071	0.1
Culture and art	403	1.1	3'241	0.8	98'786	0.7
Science and science services	268	0.7	3'006	0.7	91'420	0.7
Finance, credit, insurance, pensions	221	0.6	1'080	0.3	403'559	3
Total	**37'660**	**100**	**423'813**	**100**	**13'649'155**	**100**

Source: Ministry of Statistics and Analysis, 2007.

According to the Ministry of Statistics, however, among the most profitable activities for small enterprises in Belarus are real estate, communications and material supply and sales. They all display profitability levels between 26 and 45 per cent but a low contribution to total output and employment. Among the activities that contribute the most to total output, only trade and catering boasts profitability levels above 20 per cent.

Official data also show a concentration of small business activity in the region and the city of Minsk, reflecting the higher economic development levels of the region. In 2006, 46 per cent of SMEs and 42 per cent of SME employees were in Minsk City. The figures increase to 59 per cent and 55 per cent, respectively, when the entire Minsk region is considered. As mentioned in chapter II, in order to rebalance economic development differentials in Belarus, the government has recently introduced a programme to attract investment to small cities and villages. It is too early, however, to assess the effectiveness of the programme.

In terms of tax revenues, at the end of 2007, small enterprises and individual entrepreneurs accounted respectively for 11.5 per cent and 3 per cent of the total tax revenues in Belarus,[76] which is well below their percentage contribution to total GDP.

C. SME policies, programmes, institutions and initiatives in Belarus

In addition to the overall objectives and measures on SME development, as outlined in the Programme of Social and Economic Development of the Republic of Belarus for 2006–2010 (section A), there are a number of policies and programmes in place that provide more details on how these objectives will be achieved. Over recent years, the public–private dialogue on issues related to entrepreneurship development has become more intense and the authorities are implementing changes that frequently address, directly or indirectly, at least some of the concerns expressed by the business community. This section briefly reviews the most relevant initiatives to foster the development of the SME sector undertaken by the government and other organizations, including both public and private SME support institutions.

I. Key SME policies and programmes

State Programme of Support to Small Business

The State Programme of Support to Small Business consists of a programmatic document adopted annually that includes objectives as well as a range of measures to achieve the SME development goals outlined in the broader Programme of Social and Economic Development of the Republic of Belarus for 2006–2010 (box III.2).

The 2009 State Programme of Support to Small Business was approved by the Decision of the Council of Ministers 65 of 2009. The programme contains policy guidelines aimed at promoting favourable conditions for the sustainable development of small businesses including:

- Improving the legislation regulating small businesses;
- Facilitating the provision of financial support to small businesses;
- Improving the support infrastructure for SMEs;
- Developing linkages between small businesses and large enterprises;
- Promoting small business in small and medium cities and rural areas;
- Providing for SME training and retraining;
- Improving information for small businesses;
- Promoting international cooperation and the development of SMEs' foreign trade activities.

The programme will be funded from different sources including the state and local budgets as well as bank credits. Through the programme, the government aims to increase the share of the SME sector in both total revenue from the sale of goods and services and in total employment to 18.5 per cent.

---

[76] Ministry of Foreign Affairs and Ministry of Economy (2008).

Box III.2. Measures to achieve the projected parameters
of SME development by 2010 (2006–2010)

In 2006, the Council of Ministers adopted a set of measures aimed at achieving the SME development targets of the Programme of Social and Economic Development by 2010. These measures include:

- **Organizational measures**: drafting of basic forecast on SME development by the Council of Ministers; developing regional or sectoral action plans on SME development; adopting key measures for SME development including on job creation; preparation of information on key SME performance indicators; and developing and adopting decisions relating to regional socio-economic development (2006–2010);

- **Improving the legal and regulatory framework**: simplifying administrative procedures; expanding access to credit and finance for SMEs; compensating SMEs for interest on bank loans and foreign credit lines for investment projects; developing and implementing measures to gradually reduce the scope of price control; and simplifying state registration, licensing and fiscal regulation;

- **Simplified system of taxation for SMEs**: a simplified taxation system for SMEs (chapter II); a simplified accounting system; and the tax base of retail, catering and transport SMEs will be calculated based on actual income;

- **Improving real estate support to SME**: transfer and sale of unused property in certain areas for specific investment projects; direct sale to investors of companies working at a loss for a period of three years; budget loans to promote leasing system to SMEs; and granting of real estate property in exchange for an agreement to create new jobs;

- **Improving infrastructure support to SMEs**: preparing draft regulations/acts governing the activities of core business support centres; developing basic business support centres; creating infrastructure to support the creation of new SMEs; introducing new production technologies; and facilitating access to international markets;

- **Development of industrial cooperation between SMEs and other enterprises**: analyzing industrial cooperation between SMEs and other enterprises; analyzing international best practice of industrial cooperation; creating a subcontracting centre; and proposing measures to stimulate industrial cooperation;

- **Cooperation with non-profit organizations**: conferences, seminars, roundtables and meetings with business experts from non-profit organizations;

- **Improving information support for SMEs**: providing media coverage on SME development; preparing, publishing and disseminating statistical information on the development of SMEs; developing information and marketing systems to improve access of SMEs to information databases, e-commerce opportunities, etc; and organizing annual competitions (e.g. best exporter of the year);

- **Training for SMEs**: organizing training seminars including cross-border projects to exchange information; improving the system of education and training and retraining on entrepreneurship; and programmes to train entrepreneurs from the unemployed;

- **International cooperation and SMEs**: increasing cooperation with foreign states and international organizations on SME development; conducting international dialogues in order to study the legal framework of other states, establish relations with foreign partners and promote products in foreign markets; developing and implementing international technical assistance projects aimed at supporting and developing the SME sector; and supporting the involvement of SMEs in international trade;

- **Monitoring**: analyzing the SME sector in order to prepare proposals on improving the support and development of the sector; and assessing SME contribution to broader economic priorities.

Source: Government of Belarus (2006). Decision of Council of Ministers 1029 of 2006.

The State Programme for Development of Regions, Small and Medium Urban Communities

The programme time frame is 2007–2010 and aims at the development of the least developed areas of Belarus, covering 187 communities.[77] Its main objectives are to implement around 1,000 investment projects (including 195 priority projects) that will create over 19,000 new jobs, reduce unemployment to 1 per cent and improve living standards. State support will be provided to enterprises to raise their competitiveness and promote a favourable environment for small businesses.

Moreover, as mentioned in chapter II, a special tax regime became effective in 2008. It applies to both foreign and Belarusian legal entities and individual entrepreneurs located in rural areas as well as town centres (populated by less than 50,000 persons and included in a list prepared by the Council of Ministers) that carry out business activities involving the manufacture of goods, performance of works or provision of services.

The National Innovation Development Programme for 2007–2010

Approved by Presidential Decree 136 of 2007, the National Innovation Development Programme[78] consists primarily of a fund for innovation aimed at creating 100 new companies and 386 modern production facilities, modernizing 609 companies and introducing 888 new high technologies, in what appears to be a very ambitious set of objectives. Elaborated by the State Committee for Science and Technology with the participation of all ministries and regional authorities, the programme plans to focus research and development activities until 2010 on resource- and energy-saving technologies and on the production of competitive products.

A major goal is to increase the share of new industrial products to 19 per cent by 2010 from 10.4 per cent in 2006 and the share of innovative companies to 25 per cent from 14.1 per cent in 2006. In addition, over 2,000 enterprises will undergo certification for compliance with the ISO 9001 international standards.[79] The estimated budget is BYR 15.8 trillion and the Ministry of Economy, Ministry of Finance, regional administrations and the Minsk City Hall are expected to map out the financial resources necessary for its implementation. Despite the fact that SMEs are generally active subjects of innovation activities, there is no clear indication that these are a target group for the programme.

The Belarusian Fund for Financial Support to Entrepreneurs

The fund was created in 1992 (Decision of the Council of Ministers 36 of 1992) and now operates in accordance with Presidential Decree 136 of 1998, which introduced its regulations. The primary objectives of the fund[80] are to provide financial resources for implementation of the State Programme of Support to Small Business and to extend financing to investment projects directed at the creation, restructuring or technical re-equipment of SMEs.

To achieve the above objectives, the fund provides SMEs with credits and property on lease. In the course of 2008, 52 such investment projects were financed through the fund, for a total of BYR 2.2 billion (around $767,000). The government reports that 187 new jobs were created as a result.

The European Bank for Reconstruction and Development (EBRD) is also providing Belarusian SMEs with assistance in the area of access to finance (box III.3).

---

[77] http://w3.economy.gov.by/ministry/economy.nsf/c0f0523c581097c9c225701900349321/e71ee324b0aa2ab2c22573ec004e99c4/$FILE/Programma.doc
[78] http://www.levonevski.net/pravo/razdel5/num2/5d25216.html
[79] http://www.Government.by/en/eng_solution2541.html
[80] http://w3.economy.gov.by/ministry/economy.nsf/dd5cab6801f1723585256474005327c8/1f59982e12319b9ec2256d18002af34e?OpenDocument

Box III.3. The European Bank for Reconstruction and Development and access to finance in Belarus

In December 2004, the EBRD signed an SME support framework aimed at supporting the development of the private sector in Belarus and providing credit lines to new private banks.[81] The first allocation of $25 million consisted of senior loans to commercial banks in Belarus. Under this framework, loans were extended directly to the participating local banks, which on-lent the funds to private micro, small and medium-sized enterprises. Two banks – Belgazprombank and Priorbank (Raiffeisen) – participated in the framework. In January 2007, an extension of the framework for an additional $25 million (framework II) was approved by the EBRD.

In July 2007, the EBRD Board of Directors approved a facility to Priorbank comprising (a) a $20 million SME credit line including an A loan of up to $15 million for the bank's account and (b) a commercial syndicated A/B loan of up to $50 million of which up to $17 million would be for the bank's account. The facility is intended to strengthen the ability of the private sector bank to expand its operations, including in the micro and SME sector in Belarus, and to facilitate Priorbank's access to international debt markets.[82]

Finally, EBRD is also implementing a project to establish a dedicated greenfield microfinance bank with co-financiers. The project will support the development of private micro and small enterprises in Belarus by providing financial services on a sustainable basis particularly in regions outside of the capital. The proposed transaction comprises a €2.5 million equity investment and a senior loan of up to €10 million for on-lending to micro and small enterprises.[83] The project is expected to have a significant impact by accelerating the development of micro and small enterprises in Belarus and by demonstrating the viability of micro and small enterprise lending operations to other local banks.

Source: EBRD.

2. SME support infrastructure

Since the mid-1990s, one of the basic directions of the state support to small business in Belarus has been the development of a public SME support infrastructure. This is aimed at assisting SMEs in all phases of their entrepreneurial activities, from start-up to financial independence. Non-state bodies also provide support services of various kinds to entrepreneurial activities and SMEs. The following provides a brief overview of the organizations and services made available:

- **Centres for Support of Entrepreneurship**. First created in 1993, the centres are public support agencies providing information and consultancy services including advice on establishing (including registration) and managing a small business; preparation of business plans; assistance in obtaining credit; assistance in conducting market research; support for training; facilitation of participation of small businesses in exhibitions and fairs; and assistance in the search for potential investors and sources of financing for investment projects.[84] As of 1 January 2009, there were 43 such centres. In 2008 alone, these offered their services to more than 20,000 people in about 800 seminars on various aspects of doing business in Belarus;

- **Business incubators**. They are entrepreneurship support facilities designed to foster a favourable environment for the operation and development of SMEs. In this respect, incubators provide SMEs with leased premises equipped for offices and production. They also offer a variety of other supporting services, such as providing SMEs with various information, consulting and sectoral services and

---

[81] http://www.ebrd.org/country/country/belarus/showcase.htm
[82] http://www.ebrd.com/about/strategy/minutes/070710.pdf
[83] http://www.ebrd.com/projects/psd/psd2007/36574.htm
[84] http://w3.economy.gov.by/ministry/economy.nsf/dd5cab6801f1723585256474005327c8/3334287b62328ed2c2256c950033af32?OpenDocument

assistance in staff training, access to finance, the search for partners and the use of new technologies. In 2008, the seven incubators' premises hosted 235 small businesses with more than 2,500 employees;

• **The Belarusian Chamber of Commerce and Industry** is described as both a public and non-governmental organization and aims to protect the interests of Belarusian businesspeople as well as foreign businesspeople based in Belarus.[85] Its main objective is to promote the development of the economy including cooperation with other countries. Its members include over 1,400 enterprises and organizations, public and private as well as domestic and foreign. It provides consulting, information and mediatory services including assisting enterprises in locating partners for direct contracts and industrial cooperation (i.e. supplier linkages or subcontracting);

• Established in 1991, the **Belarusian Union of Entrepreneurs** has more than 17,000 members, including 800 active members among heads of corporations, individual entrepreneurs, economists and journalists, who actively participate in business support programmes as experts. It has representatives in Minsk and in all regions of the Republic of Belarus;[86]

• **The National Council of the Belarusian Trade Union of Entrepreneurs "Sadrusznast" ("Community")** provides support to entrepreneurial activity including troubleshooting for SMEs in their dealings with the public administration. It also assists SMEs in identifying local and foreign business partners, holds seminars and organizes international exchange programmes;[87]

• Established in 1993, the **Belarusian Confederation of Industrialists and Entrepreneurs** is a non-profit umbrella organization for 11 unions and business associations in Belarus, representing more than 5,000 enterprises and organizations. Around 80 per cent (4,000) of its members are SMEs with 70 per cent (3,500) from the private sector. Its functions include consultative services and the coordination of employers' activities;[88]

• **The Minsk Capital Association of Entrepreneurs and Employers** is a non-governmental non-profit organization established in 1997.[89] It unites 580 members including owners, directors and leading specialists of stockholding, private, foreign and joint companies from Minsk and its region. Its aim is to establish a favourable business network where enterprises and entrepreneurs can develop and strengthen their activities. It acts as an information network with over 15,000 partners. The organization has also established a subcontracting centre (see below). One of the most prominent activities of the organization is the coordination and drafting of the National Business Platform (box III.4);

• **The Business Union of Entrepreneurs and Employers** is a non-governmental non-profit organization established in 1999.[90] The main goal of the union is to coordinate entrepreneurial activities and protect the interests of members. Half of its members are SMEs. It has established numerous functional councils in a variety of areas (e.g. tax and pricing legislation; competitiveness; regional development; labour and social relations; administrative procedures; and SME development) that interact with intersectoral commissions and working groups at the Council of Ministers;

• The **Republican Confederation of Entrepreneurship** was established in 2007. It is the largest business association in Belarus. It was initiated by the Minsk Capital Association of Entrepreneurs and Employers, the Business Union of Entrepreneurs and Employers, regional business associations of Brest, Grodno, Mogilev, Vitebsk, and the Republican trade union Sadrusznast as well as a number of other associations. One of the most important activities of the Confederation is its support to the development of the National Business Platform;

---

[85] http://www.cci.by/

[86] http://bae.iatp.by/english.htm

[87] http://www.fpb.by/ru/menu_left/organization/r_komitet/brk_sadrugnast

[88] http://www.bnpa.info/en/

[89] http://allminsk.biz/

[90] http://www.bspn.nsys.by/

- The web-based business portal bel.biz[91] was created in 2005 by the IFC with the financial assistance of the Swedish International Development Cooperation Agency and in cooperation with 100 partners including government, consulting companies, banks and business associations. The portal aims at assisting SMEs by providing information on establishing and operating companies, management, access to finance, leasing, marketing and other practical information. It provides up-to-date legal and regulatory information and practical advice on creating, financing and operating a business.[92]

Box III.4. The National Business Platform

Coordinated by the Minsk Capital Association of Entrepreneurs and Employers, the National Business Platform is a tool for representing and defending the interests of the business community through advocacy, which is considered a new phenomenon in Belarus.[93] The National Business Platform document is developed through the open dialogue of thousands of people including representatives from business, government and the wider public and is presented to the government. The first National Business Platform document was drafted early 2006. Since 2006, it has been adopted on an annual basis. Each National Business Platform contains a comprehensive set of proposals on the reform of the legislation system, administrative procedures and other state measures in order to enhance investments, foster the competitiveness of the economy and create new jobs.

The National Business Platform of 2008 proposed repealing the Golden Share Rule and prohibiting confiscation in extrajudicial procedures.[94] The priorities of the current National Business Platform (2009) include competitiveness and innovation; protection of property rights; development of market institutions; and reforms relating to taxes, licensing, certification, sanctions, penalties and registration. The main aims of the platform are institutional development, macroeconomic stability, improving the efficiency of commodity markets, improving access to finance, increasing technological readiness, encouraging innovation and promoting business excellence. Among 130 proposals it names abolishing price control, simplifying administrative procedures, enhancing transparency and adopting competition law.[95]

The platform defines tools and instruments for its implementation including: preparing bills and amendments to existing laws and regulations and submitting these to the government; consultations with government authorities and establishing links with members of parliament, the government, individual ministries and departments; harmonizing the positions of business through consultations and round tables, interviews, public and corporate dialogue; organizing focus groups to assess the views of entrepreneurs on legislative initiatives; anti-corruption initiatives; supporting entrepreneurs in disputes and in cases of unlawful imposition of sanctions; a media campaign in support of legislative initiatives; wide dissemination of information resources to protect the interests of business; enhancing partnership and cooperation between government, business organizations, the private sector, etc. on the implementation of the platform; and the use of international institutions for the promotion of national business interests.

Source: Minsk Capital Association of Entrepreneurs and Employees.

The United Nations Development Programme (UNDP) office in Belarus has been instrumental in launching a number of programmes and initiatives to promote the development of SMEs and entrepreneurship in the country since 1997, including many of those described above (see box III.5).

---

[91] http://www.bel.biz

[92] http://www.ifc.org/ifcext/eca.nsf/AttachmentsByTitle/BelBEE_SS.pdf/$FILE/BelBEE_Ss.pdf

[93] http://allminsk.biz/images/stories/adab/nbp2008.doc

[94] http://allminsk.biz/content/blogcategory/56/117/

[95] http://allminsk.biz/content/view/62/74/

Box III.5. UNDP projects and initiatives for SME development in Belarus

The UNDP office in Belarus has been promoting SME development since 1997. Initial UNDP efforts succeeded in the creation of the first business incubators and credit unions, as well as in introducing microfinance as a new mechanism to support micro business and individual entrepreneurs. A second generation of SME support activities (2002–2006) sought to facilitate public–private dialogue and partnerships by bringing together government, business associations and international organizations, including the World Bank and the IFC, to promote an environment conducive to the development of the private sector.

In 2007, in collaboration with the Council for Enterprise Development, a joint project was launched to deepen PPPs; identify and remove barriers and challenges to SME development; strengthen the expertise of the business community and broaden its options for participation in the policy and rule-making process. It is also aimed at introducing new forms of business networking and cooperation, such as subcontracting and industrial clustering. The sustained dialogue among the business community and national and local governments promoted by UNDP has led to favourable changes in the legislation that regulates business activities in areas such as taxation and accounting for SME, customs clearance, application of sanctions and fines, and manufactures' eligibility for incentives. Today, UNDP continues its activities in support of SME and entrepreneurship development. Key ongoing projects include:

1. **Improving the Administrative and Economic Environment for Private Sector Development by Facilitating Public–Private Dialogue (2007–2009)**. The project helps develop the tools for comprehensive and consistent monitoring of trends in the small business sector. It strengthens the role of the business community in creating a more favourable business environment by promoting its participation in the drafting of legislation and the development and promotion of legal initiatives;

2. **Strengthening the National System for Technology Transfer on the Basis of ICT (2006–2009)**. The project facilitates the development of private enterprise based on technological innovation by working to (a) improve the legal and institutional framework for technology transfer and raise the status of intellectual property rights in the evaluation and transfer of technologies; (b) support innovation-driven enterprises among young people; and (c) encourage technology foresight surveys;

3. **Fostering Public-Private Partnerships and Promoting Corporate Social Responsibility (2008–2009)**. As an integral part of the relevant regional initiative, the project aims to raise public awareness of the United Nations Global Compact and build business commitment to adopt corporate social responsibility and promote PPPs; to launch the national Global Compact chapter and establish the local Global Compact network; and to create particular public–private partnerships;

4. **Supporting Microfinance Development (2008–2010)**. The project is designed to mobilize the efforts of the government, finance and credit institutions, international organizations and enterprise support associations with a view to improving access to microfinance services for the general public and particularly for small business;

5. **Promoting Private Sector Activity in the Regions by Enhancing Capacity of Small Business Development Centres (2008–2010)**. The project seeks to build capacity and enhance capabilities of the SME support infrastructure to better serve new business start-ups and to improve working practices vis-à-vis small business development and self-employment, particularly in rural areas. The project will work on developing, testing and adapting market-driven approaches within the SME support infrastructure, strengthening the knowledge base for the provision of advisory services and consultancies to business start-ups and creating demonstration business models to be tested in small towns and rural areas of the Mogilev, Brest and Minsk oblasts.

Source: UNDP (2005).

3. Specific initiatives to develop the SME sector

High technology parks

On 22 September 2005, the President of Belarus signed a decree on high technology parks. The decree aims at boosting competitiveness by developing new and high technology sectors. In 2006, the high technology park was registered as a state-owned legal entity. Its aim is to become the Belarusian "Silicon Valley" with a territory of 500 thousand square metres and featuring a tailor-made legal regime that will remain in effect for 15 years after the decree comes into force. For the moment, all Belarusian legal entities – including those with 100 per cent foreign investment – and individual entrepreneurs whose activities are concerned with development and software support of information system and data processing activities can become residents of the high technology park regardless of their physical location. Park residents are exempt from a variety of taxes, levies and other payments to government (see chapter II). The high technology park provides premises for both domestic and foreign innovative and high technology enterprises including SMEs.

Linkages support

In transitional economies such as the Czech Republic, Hungary and Poland, outsourcing and subcontracting have created significant opportunities for SMEs to contribute to increased employment and competitiveness. However, in Belarus outsourcing and subcontracting are much less common for SMEs. SMEs generally compete with each other in the production of finished goods. Consequently, many SMEs lack the opportunity to specialize and innovate that is typically associated with outsourcing and subcontracting, particularly by TNCs. As a result, there is limited business-to-business cooperation that intensifies the problems of inadequate capital and other constraints faced by SMEs in gaining access to markets. Consequently, SMEs tend to focus on activities that require limited investment.

In Belarus, the terms "supplier linkages" or "subcontracting" are more commonly referred to as "industrial (or manufacturing) cooperation". Both the Council of Minsters Resolution 1029 of 2006 and the 2006 Programme of State Support of Small Businesses include measures on the development of mechanisms for industrial cooperation between SMEs and other enterprises including the establishment of a subcontracting centre to provide information databases on enterprises (needs or goods and services offered) and match SMEs with other enterprises to promote higher productivity through greater division of labour and specialization.[96]

The Minsk Capital Association of Entrepreneurs and Employers has established a subcontracting centre that is part of a regional network of 35 subcontracting centres under the Interregional Centre of Industrial Subcontracting and Partnership based in Moscow.[97] The latter is made up of mainly regional centres in the Russian Federation but also includes subcontracting centres in Belarus, Latvia and Ukraine. The Belarus subcontracting centre is independent from the government and provides information on proposals (supply) and requests (orders), and suppliers and buyers. In addition, it provides training and organizes conferences on subcontracting. The centre receives 200–300 requests per week, the vast majority of which originate from large foreign firms (95 per cent).

In addition, the Department of Entrepreneurship and the Minsk business incubator MAP ZAO established a subcontracting centre providing information on proposals and requests. MAP ZAO also administers a website on subcontracting opportunities in Belarus.[98] The website subcontract.by includes a database of firms and their production capabilities. However, these are dominated by firms with over 250 employees and few SMEs (according to either Belarus or EU definitions of small enterprises or SMEs). Other associations such as the Belarusian Chamber of Commerce and Industry also provide matchmaking services.

At present, only a few large Belarusian enterprises concentrated mainly in automotives and machinery have established supplier linkages with local SMEs. These include the Minsk Automobile Plant, Minsk Machinery Factory, Belarusian Automobile Factory and Minsk Tractor Works. In addition, there is limited evidence of foreign investors using local suppliers except for basic intermediate inputs such as cartons and boxes.

---

[96] Decision of the Council of Ministers 128 of 2006; Decision of Council of Ministers 1029 of 2006.

[97] http://minsk.subcontract.ru/Partner/default.html and http://allminsk.biz

[98] http://subcontract.by

D. A strategy to support SME development through FDI

Section A of this chapter outlines the channels through which FDI can contribute to the development of the productive sector in a host country as well as the factors influencing a country's ability to maximize its benefits. In Belarus, as described in sections B and C, many policies and institutions have been established with the explicit objective of fostering SMEs and entrepreneurship. For the time being, however, the SME sector remains at very early stages of development, both in terms of its contribution to total GDP and employment, and of its integration into the supply chains of local and foreign investors. Thus, the sector's ability to reap the benefits of foreign investment remains very limited. FDI can and could be better utilized to contribute to the development of the sector, but to reach this objective, a more decisive stance towards reducing the constraints to SME development as well as more targeted policy initiatives are needed.

This section outlines the key elements of a strategy to support SME development in Belarus by making better use of FDI. These comprise first and foremost improving the investment climate. This would not only help attract FDI but would also be beneficial for all local and foreign businesses including SMEs. Addressing the shortcomings of the investment climate is a necessary precondition to unleash local entrepreneurship and foster the development of a competitive Belarusian private sector. Therefore, an important leap in competitiveness and capacity is required if local SMEs are to share the gains from FDI. The reason, as discussed in the first section of this chapter, is twofold: on the one hand, local SMEs willing to participate in the supply chain of the TNCs will be requested to display high levels of productivity and cost efficiency; on the other, the capacity of the local SMEs to successfully face the competition of TNCs, absorb new technology and production techniques and access new markets through FDI will depend on their levels of efficiency and technological distance from the TNCs.

The strategy proposed in this section also recommends a set of more targeted policy interventions to foster the developmental role of FDI for the sector, such as attracting FDI to specific sectors via investor targeting policies, strengthening local absorptive capacity and designing specific linkages policies. Each element should form part of an integrated and coherent approach, implemented by mutually reinforcing policies, as depicted in figure III.1 and further discussed below (UNCTAD, forthcoming a).

Figure III.1. A systemic approach to attract FDI and support SME development

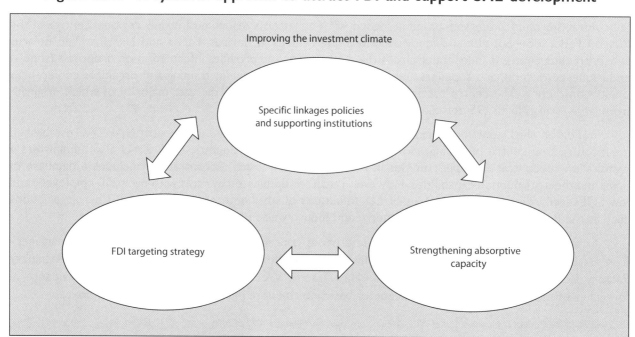

Source: UNCTAD, adaptation from Altenburg (2000).

1. Improving the investment climate to support SME development and FDI attraction

As mentioned throughout this report, recent reforms by the Government of Belarus have gone some way towards reducing the regulatory and administrative constraints to doing business, including by streamlining the business registration process, abolishing the Golden Share Rule, simplifying the tax system for SMEs and introducing new incentive schemes to attract investment in underdeveloped areas of the country (chapter II). However, further improvements to the legal and regulatory framework for business are needed to make Belarus a more attractive destination for FDI across different sectors of the economy at levels that would spur the emergence of business linkages and generate significant spillover effects.

The second chapter of this report has identified a number of elements and concrete recommendations on how to improve the regulatory framework for FDI as well as domestic investors. Most hurdles affecting foreign investors and large companies apply also to SMEs, with the aggravation that these companies are generally less equipped to face them, both in terms of financial and human capital resources.

In addition, Belarusian SMEs face a range of regulatory and non-regulatory difficulties that are sector specific and contribute to maintaining it at the lowest levels of development in the region. The compounded effect is a reduction in the competitiveness of the Belarusian SME sector, which limits the insertion of Belarusian products into international markets and the scope for the establishment of supplier linkages with existing and potential foreign investors in the country. The key constraints are described below along with recommendations to reduce them.

Level and administration of taxes

The Belarusian tax system is particularly onerous for SMEs since even the smallest company requires at least one full-time accountant. As explored in chapter II, the government is actively working towards a simplification of the system. In order to alleviate the tax burden on SMEs and reduce the administrative requirements for tax filing, Presidential Edict 119 of 2007 introduced a Simplified System of Taxation for small enterprises. This provides an option to substitute the payment of most taxes and dues[99] with a tax on gross revenue of 8 per cent or 10 per cent (box II.4 in chapter II for further details). These rates are still high and burdensome for many producers. It is thus recommended that the government evaluate the effectiveness of this incentive scheme in achieving its objective, i.e. fostering SME development and expanding the tax base. Taking in due consideration the potential fiscal revenue loss involved, it should consider whether a reduction in the tax rates of the Simplified System of Taxation is needed.

Price controls

Comprehensive price legislation is accompanied by high penalties for its violation and it is not surprising that price regulations rank high among the problems affecting the Belarusian SME sector.[100] As seen in chapter II, the authorities control prices by directly setting their level (such as for "socially important" products), by fixing maximum price increase indexes (such as the monthly price increase cap of 0.5 per cent above which any company must receive approval by the authorities[101]) or by establishing the methods of price settings. All enterprises are obliged to provide economic justification of prices and calculations in special forms provided by law (GET/IPM, 2007).

Price controls are intended to "pursue a balanced pricing policy based on optimal combinations of the mechanisms of state regulation and free price formation".[102] In reality, however, apart from creating

---

99   With the exception of the VAT (if employing more than 15 persons), import and export taxes, the state duty, the offshore due, the taxes on income from securities operations, the obligatory insurance dues and other social security protection.

100   In a 2007 survey by the IPM Research Centre, price ranked fourth among the obstacles for the SME sector in Belarus (GET/IPM, 2007).

101   Resolution of the Council of Minister 944 of 1999, Regulation of the Council of Ministers of 30 December 2006 on Some Measures on Securing the Predictive Inflation Indicator in 2007, reconfirmed in the letter of the Ministry of Economy 481 of March 2008 on the Limit of Price Increase.

102   http://www.belarus.by/en/belarus/economy/macroeconomic/liberalisation/

distortions in the allocation of resources that affect all economic agents, price controls have a number of negative impacts that are more accentuated for SMEs. These include the time and resources lost in the preparation of cost information reports, the registration of new prices and the preparation of routine calculations, often requiring recourse to specialists to avoid the fines imposed by improper implementation of the regulations. For instance, an enterprise exceeding the allowed price increase without registering the new price will have the additional income confiscated and pay a penalty corresponding to twice the additional turnover (IPM, 2008).

A 2006 survey on the impact of price controls on the Belarusian SME sector estimated that, on average, 2.75 workers per company deal with the calculation of costs, price setting and registration with the relevant governmental bodies. Each of them spends about 46 hours per month (six working days) performing these functions. Price deregulation could therefore lead to an annual cost savings of about $10,000 for an average SME (GET/IPM, 2007). Another pernicious effect of price controls is that it discourages the creation of linkages between local SMEs and foreign companies, to which such controls do not apply.

In an attempt to support private sector development, in February 2008, Resolution of the Council of Ministers 252 freed individual entrepreneurs and SMEs using the Simplified System of Taxation from compulsory registration of prices outside the established limits. Until price liberalization is achieved for all but a relatively narrow list of public goods,[103] the government should consider extending the above measure to all SMEs.

Complexity and variability of regulations, licensing and other controls

As stressed in chapter II, the regulatory framework for business in Belarus is extremely complex and subject to frequent changes. The excessive regulation of entrepreneurial activity reduces the competitiveness of the local SME sector vis-à-vis Belarus' regional competitors, fosters the development of the informal (shadow) economy and affects the establishment of supplier linkages. Moreover, the multitude of administrative procedures and regulations create a nourishing environment for rent-seeking behaviour in the public sector and state bureaucracy.

Since 2006 significant progress has been made with respect to controls and inspections, yet entrepreneurial activity in Belarus remains the object of a high number of administrative controls (as discussed in chapter II), which result in high violation and penalization rates. In 2006, for example, more than 42 per cent of SMEs were found in violation of the legislation and more than 52 per cent of these were fined (IFC, 2008). The 2008 IFC study (see chapter II) suggests a number of reforms to the inspection system, which this report endorses. These include the simplification of existing legislation, improved coordination among inspecting agencies, the introduction of consultative services for SMEs, the elimination of unscheduled inspections and the re-alignment of sanctions to reflect the gravity of the violations. In addition, inspections should be targeted at high risk cases rather than all enterprises.

Lack of commercial mindset

According to many investors, the complexity of the business environment reflects, and is sometimes the result of, the scepticism of many public administration representatives regarding private sector entrepreneurial activities. The state is considered as the key agent and manager of nearly all economic processes in the country and the main source of employment and services. As stressed in the chapter II, private investors lament discrimination in the access to raw materials and inputs between private companies and SOEs, particularly with respect to access to construction materials. SMEs attribute the lack of supplier linkages with large SOEs to low levels of trust between government and the private sector. Such a cultural

---

[103] While regulation of prices can be justified in certain specific cases such as key essential goods, economic theory cannot justify the broad-based predetermination of prices.

bias is one of the factors behind the persisting constraints against SME development described in this chapter.

However, as discussed in the previous chapters of this report, over the last two years it is possible to observe a change in the state approach towards entrepreneurship as expressed in the declarations and statements of high-level policymakers such as the President, the President of the National Bank and ministers in the Ministry of Economy. For instance, the President of Belarus stressed that "the period when the economy operated in manual mode has finished [... and] existing laws and regulations require simplification, streamlining and stability".[104] The Chairperson of the National Bank expressed the need to create conditions to facilitate business and investment by dismantling the existing bureaucracy through reviewing the regulatory framework and repealing outdated rules.[105] Nevertheless, as stressed in the preceding chapters of this report, unless the new approach is consistently shared by the entire administration, it will remain difficult to accelerate the development of the private sector including SMEs.

Reporting to government agencies

As stressed in chapter II, all companies in Belarus are subject to extensive and resource-intensive reporting requirements from a range of government agencies. Once more, this appears particularly burdensome for SMEs. An IPM study suggests that a typical SME uses on average 3.14 employees to prepare the necessary reports to administrative bodies and that the executive of a typical SME spends more than 9 hours per week communicating with administrative agents, which costs on average $420 per month in wages (IPM, 2007).[106] These are direct costs borne by SMEs to pay wages to unproductive employees. Costs related to unnecessary reporting are also incurred by the state and therefore the taxpayer. Rationalization and de-bureaucratization have begun and the government is considering the use of electronic filing; however, a dramatic revision of the reporting requirements of all agencies at the central and local levels of the administration is necessary.

Education and business skills

The educational system is one of the key determinants of competitiveness in Belarus. Belarus has indeed achieved high levels of literacy and technical expertise. However, like in most other transition economies, the education system has for long been biased towards sciences and engineering, neglecting social sciences, law and business skills, although the number of business and law graduates has been increasing in recent years.

Fostering private sector development in the Belarusian economy requires a re-orientation of educational profiles. Education in business skills, especially entrepreneurship, is required at secondary schools and universities as well as vocational training and lifelong education. Entrepreneurs need to focus their learning on the internal determinants of competitiveness by improving their knowledge of marketing, management, quality consciousness and environment management.

To accelerate the supply of executive talents in the medium term, the government should consider establishing a joint venture business school. Management education is globalizing rapidly and given the Belarusian context, there is an urgent requirement to improve the quantity and quality of management education to support SME development and FDI attraction over the short to medium term. A new privately-funded world-class business school with competitive entry in collaboration with an internationally renowned overseas partner should be established. The new business school could operate outside the programmatic constraints imposed by the present structures and regulations for public universities. The key issue is the

---

[104] Statement made on the 13th November 2007. http://www.president.gov.by/press44843.print.html
[105] Statement made on the 13th November 2007. http://www.president.gov.by/press44843.print.html
[106] http://research.by/rus/surveys/ba8c266b453d0117.html

selection of a partner institution: an obvious target could be one of the elite European or North American business schools, a number of which are active globally and should at least be considered. There is, however, an argument for evaluating a world-class business school already based in a transition economy as the desired target for collaboration, given the greater familiarity with business practices in the Belarusian context.

2.   Attracting FDI to specific sectors

There are several characteristics of the Belarusian economy that make it a potentially attractive destination for FDI. These include a sizeable internal market, a privileged location between the European Union and the Russian Federation that makes the country a natural transport corridor, a well-developed transport infrastructure and a highly skilled (and relatively cheap) labour force with particular expertise in science and technology (especially information technology (IT)). Last, but not least, the country's commitment to reforms, which, if sustained, will certainly contribute to increasing its attractiveness vis-à-vis foreign investors.

So far, as highlighted in chapter I, Belarus has underperformed in attracting FDI. This relates to the challenging investment climate but also to the country's international image as a fundamentally state-run economy with little scope for private investment. Provided progress in the reform agenda continues, and the global economy recovers from the current economic crisis, Belarus will perforce attract more FDI. This will occur even if no further improvements take place in specific programmes to promote FDI and facilitate its entry. Professional investment promotion, however, can speed up the change in perceptions about Belarus as an investment location by effectively channelling relevant business environment information to overseas investors and helping direct FDI to the sectors and activities where it is most needed.

Investment promotion in Belarus has been a limited undertaking until recently. The National Investment Agency, the country's official IPA, was too small to carry out the typical range of functions of a modern IPA. Its seven staff members (out of which three administrative officers), although dynamic and motivated, focused primarily on facilitating investors' scoping missions to the country and acting as mediators (troubleshooting) between investors and the public administration when specific problems arose. Other typical and equally important functions of an IPA, such as investor targeting, aftercare, advocacy and image building have been carried out only on a non-systematic basis due to human capital as well as financial constraints.

Since 2008, however, the government has started boosting its investment promotion efforts. The organization of the Belarus Investment Forum in London in November 2008 is a recent example (box III.6). In parallel, the authorities are considering an overhaul of the institutional setting for investment promotion. According to a draft decree of the President, a reorganization of the National Investment Agency should take place in 2009. Accordingly, the regular staff of the agency should increase and the agency would report directly to the Prime Minister's office (currently the agency reports to the Ministry of Economy). The new agency should be established in the course of 2009, with technical assistance from the Turkish IPA.

According to the draft decree, the main tasks of the new agency are to provide investors with consulting services and facilitate their communication at all levels of the administration (facilitation), prepare suggestions to the Prime Minister for improving the legislation regulating investment activity (advocacy), create and manage a database of investment activities (which could be used for aftercare activities) and organize presentations on the investment potential of Belarus and its investment climate (marketing).

Box III.6. Attracting foreign investors – the first Belarus Investment Forum

In an effort to promote the investment potential of the country and improve its image as an ideal location for foreign investors, the Government of Belarus organized an investment forum in November 2008. The event took place in London and attracted more than 500 participants, including high-level government officials, senior business executives from across Europe and high-ranking representatives from national and international organizations.

Led by the Prime Minister, the government delegation informed foreign investors about investment opportunities in Belarus. The government representatives also provided information about the conditions for doing business in the country and measures recently taken to create a favourable investment climate. In addition to the plenary session, the forum was also an opportunity to present and to hold bilateral discussions on specific investment projects with the potential to attract foreign investment.

Stimulated by the success of this first investment forum, the Government of Belarus is contemplating the idea of organizing such events in other parts of the world.

Source: UNCTAD.

These are all encouraging developments that should bring investment promotion in Belarus closer to international best practice. In particular, the facilitation role assigned to the new IPA goes in the direction recommended in the second chapter of this report, which advises assigning the national IPA a troubleshooting role between investors and the regions with regard to the emergence of roadblocks to investment at the local level. However, there is scope, without undue budget cost, to further shape Belarus' FDI stimulation programmes to both accelerate FDI inflows and target areas of FDI that will have the greatest developmental impact. In this respect, it is recommended that the new IPA be mandated and adequately equipped to carry out proactive sectoral investor targeting.

Naturally, the selection of a pilot sector (subsectors) for FDI targeting will depend on numerous factors specific to the local environment (e.g. the extent to which local capacity can produce at the levels required by TNCs). Despite the importance of the local context, in the early stages, the targeting activity should be aimed at attracting investors in those sectors and activities most likely to generate linkages with the local economic agents. International experience may be helpful in indicating particular sectors and activities with a propensity for backward linkages. These include the automobile industry, IT supporting services and high technology equipment, light industry (e.g. household goods, largely finished products), the garment industry, food processing, chemicals, pharmaceuticals and services (especially tourism).

Given the similarities between Belarus and some of its neighbours, it may also be useful to explore the experience of other countries in the region. There are several similarities, for instance, between Belarus and Lithuania including highly skilled labour, transition economy status, a relatively late start at privatization and low levels of FDI inflows. A survey of Lithuanian enterprises using firm-level data in the manufacturing sector[107] shows that food, beverages and tobacco attracted the largest share of FDI followed by textiles and leather products, refined petroleum products and chemicals, electrical equipment, optical instruments and wood products (Javorick, 2004).

Many of these subsectors and products typically demonstrate a tendency for backward linkages. The survey results show that the productivity of Lithuanian firms is positively correlated with the degree of potential contacts with TNCs in downstream activities.[108] The results also reveal significant evidence of

---

[107] Accounting for approximately 85 per cent of total output.

[108] Only TNCs with joint (foreign and domestic) ownership.

productivity spillovers through backward linkages in pulp, paper and paper products (17.2 per cent), basic metals (16.7 per cent), radio, television and communication equipment (14.4 per cent), wood and wood products (12.5 per cent), medical and optical instruments (11.9 per cent) and rubber and plastic products (11.0 per cent).

In Belarus, there are several sectors and activities with a high propensity for linkages including the production of tractors, chemicals, agro-processing, electronics and light industry as well as the service sector, particularly IT and software development. Many of the SOEs included in the recent phase of privatization are engaged in such activities, including food processing, light industry and high technology equipment. This provides an opportunity for the government to use the privatization programme to pilot start a full-fledged linkages programme. The company selection criteria as well as the different phases of the programme are detailed later in this section.

What is relevant, with respect to investor targeting, is that a significant effort will be required from the new National Investment Agency to produce high quality sectoral baseline information and the sectoral studies needed to present specific opportunities to target investors before the targeted promotion is launched. The effectiveness of investor targeting is in fact determined, in part, by the quality of the information and analysis used to screen the investors, sectors and projects during the various targeting steps (UNCTAD, 2008). This will mean introducing effective coordination between the National Investment Agency and other relevant ministries and government agencies that have the competences to produce such analysis, as well as building up the capacity of the National Investment Agency staff to deliver promotional information accurately and professionally.

Targeting is a strategic approach to attracting FDI through a carefully planned process that involves (UNCTAD, 2008):

1. Active identification of specific investment projects;
2. Careful planning and management of investor search programmes;
3. Investigation of specific corporate priorities;
4. Confidential promotion to specific corporate executives;
5. Delivery through a single window system of sole agency leadership, management and coordination.

UNCTAD has assisted many IPAs around the world in developing their investor targeting strategies and stands ready to provide technical assistance to the Government of Belarus in this domain.

3.   Strengthening local absorptive capacity

The creation and extent of linkages between SMEs and large domestic and foreign enterprises and the internalization of spillovers from FDI depend to a large extent on local absorptive capacity as discussed above. TNCs have the incentive to directly assist potential and existing suppliers with innovating and strengthening their competitiveness to benefit from improvements made by suppliers. However, without a sufficient level of initial absorptive capacity, competitiveness and an enabling environment for business, not only are TNCs unlikely to be willing to promote such interactions, but FDI also risks crowding out domestic firms in competing or complementary activities. In such circumstances, government interventions can play an important role in promoting the ability of firms to recognize the value of new, external information, assimilate it and apply it to commercial ends.

Once more, the development literature concurs on giving priority to the improvement of the overall enabling environment for business, as discussed above. Consequently, there are a number of targeted interventions to address incentive, information and coordination failures that the Government of Belarus could consider introducing to raise absorptive capacity, such as investing in knowledge creation and innovation infrastructure (e.g. funding of education and research system, measurement system, intellectual property agencies, standard setting) and actively promoting linkages and spillover effects through targeted programmes (UNCTAD, 2006a). In this regard, the innovation focus of the Programme of Social and Economic Development of the Republic of Belarus for 2006–2010 and the National Innovation Development Programme discussed in section C of this chapter are evidence that the government has recognized the need to foster domestic innovation and absorption capacities. The current approach to innovation, nevertheless, does not target SMEs who, in many fields, provide the channels along which new technologies develop.

Among other policies that the Government of Belarus could consider introducing in this area are:

- Opening an EMPRETEC centre in Belarus. EMPRETEC is UNCTAD's integrated entrepreneurship and innovation capacity-building programme that promotes the creation of sustainable support structures to help promising entrepreneurs build innovative and internationally competitive small and medium-sized enterprises. The programme follows a training method that focuses on the entrepreneurs, examining their personal strengths and weaknesses and working with their ability and willingness to seek and attain improved quality, productivity, growth and profitability. It encourages the entrepreneurs to be successful managers by developing their personal entrepreneurial competences. Since its inception in 1988, the EMPRETEC network has been extended to 27 countries. It now assists more than 120,000 entrepreneurs through local market-driven business support centres;

- Reducing the initial transaction costs of engaging with a research base, especially for SMEs. The innovation vouchers used in the Netherlands offer a positive example in this respect. To encourage the flow of information from knowledge institutes to SMEs, the Government of the Netherlands introduced innovation vouchers, first as a pilot project, but as of 2006 as a permanent way of promoting knowledge transfer to SMEs. Innovation vouchers enable SMEs to submit research questions to knowledge institutes, thereby encouraging meetings between the two. Vouchers are given to SMEs that need some research to innovate products, production processes or services. Every SME is entitled to a one-time "small voucher" worth €2,500. "Large vouchers" are worth €7,500 but they come with a price tag: an SME has to contribute one third of the research costs itself, while the government adds the remaining two thirds up to a maximum of €5,000. Large vouchers cover more extensive research questions. Each SME may receive a maximum of one large voucher per year;[109]

- Introducing initiatives to demonstrate the value that skilled researchers can add to a business by promoting Knowledge Transfer Partnerships. These are relationships formed between a company and an academic institution (a "Knowledge Base" partner) that facilitate the transfer of knowledge, technology and skills to which the company would not otherwise have access. Following the successful example of the United Kingdom, each partnership employs one or more recently qualified people (known as an associate) to work in a company on a project of strategic importance to the business, whilst also being supervised by the Knowledge Base partner. Since its establishment in 2003, the programme has counted more than 1,000 partnerships across the United Kingdom;[110]

- Establishing a credit guarantee fund. Limited access to finance is a major obstacle in Belarus, where no credit guarantee system exists and obtaining credit is difficult and costly. The government offers financial support to SMEs through the central and local budgets. However, resources are low and funds provided to SMEs are often small compared with the time and effort needed to obtain them (IPM, 2008). The UNDP in Belarus carried out a survey that showed that over 70 per cent of start-

---

[109] http://www.senternovem.nl/english/products_services/encouraging_innovation/innovation_vouchers.asp

[110] http://www.ktponline.org.uk/ and the presentation by Ken Warwick, of the United Kingdom Department for Trade and Industry, "The Role of Government in Building Absorptive Capacity", made at the Knowledge Economy Forum VI, April 2007, available at: http://siteresources.worldbank.org/EXTECAREGTOPKNOECO/Resources/.

up entrepreneurs rely on their own resources or those of friends or relatives and only 5 per cent of respondents accessed bank loans. Credit guarantee schemes are effective tools to assist start-up entrepreneurs to access financing by alleviating the problems of collateral security. These schemes are frequently used in advanced market economies and in developing countries and are also used to assist SMEs in their export operations.

4. Designing specific linkages policies

As described in section A of this chapter, linkages between TNCs and local firms provide a way of exchanging information, technology, skills and other assets throughout the economy. Linkages between TNCs and SMEs are "potentially one of the fastest and most effective ways of upgrading domestic enterprises, facilitating the transfer of technology, knowledge and skills, improving business and management practices, and facilitating access to finance and markets" (UNCTAD, forthcoming a). Strong linkages can increase efficiency, productivity and technological and managerial capabilities of domestic firms.

The main objective of most linkages programmes (namely, backward linkages) is to improve the capabilities of domestic enterprises to supply inputs to TNCs, which would otherwise be imported. Linkages programmes may be developed due to low levels of local capacity (e.g. inability to produce good or services of an adequate quality at the right time; substantial gaps in technological capacity between local suppliers and the needs of TNCs), where TNCs lack readily available information on local suppliers and/or where there is a lack of market diversification and internationalization of local enterprises (OECD, 2007). Appropriately designed linkages programmes can lead to the development of a dynamic, competitive and sustainable SME sector while TNCs gain access to local skills and markets. The contribution of linkages to the development of the local SME sector in Hungary is a case in point (box III.7).

Box III.7. Linkages and the development of domestic firms in Hungary

The Hungarian experience with subcontracting (linkages) was well acknowledged already in the 1970s and 1980s. Companies concluded subcontracts with more developed Western partners in order to gain access to up-to-date technology and know-how, new markets and new products. Many of them incorporated the acquired knowledge with success.

During the 1990s, subcontracting was the driving force of corporate modernization, since former development sources (primarily state subsidies) dried up. Many firms chose the new option of adjustment strategy. Hungarian companies' efforts to integrate into the international division of labour coincided with the substantial change of subcontracting deals in world markets. Subcontracting became a form of outsourcing and changed to a long-term, network type of cooperation form with considerable knowledge transfer.

Source: Szanyi (2002).

Benefits associated with linkages between domestic and foreign firms are typically greater than those among domestic firms, owing to the more extensive knowledge and skills base of many foreign firms raising the capabilities and quality to international levels more effectively than linkages among domestic firms (UNCTAD, 2001). Nevertheless, the specificity of the Belarusian environment, where traditionally very few linkages exist also among domestic firms, calls for the design of linkage policies not exclusively oriented at large TNCs, but also at those vertically integrated domestic enterprises that could benefit from a greater division of labour and competences by outsourcing parts of their supply chain operations to local SMEs.

There are several ways in which to promote local sourcing and encourage the development of the local supply base. Some of the most commonly cited methods include information and matchmaking, technology upgrading of local enterprises, training programmes with local enterprises and cluster-oriented programmes (UNCTAD, forthcoming b). As discussed in section C above, in Belarus there are currently a number of government-sponsored and private initiatives to facilitate subcontracting for SMEs. None of them, however, goes beyond matchmaking. A more comprehensive programme is needed.

In designing the linkages programme, there are a number of key elements that the government should take into consideration to ensure its efficacy and sustainability (UNCTAD, forthcoming a), including:

- **Developing a "critical mass" of buyers** to ensure sufficient demand for backward linkages to take place. It is important to have a number of buyers to avoid potential problems of unfair purchasing power by a few. These demand factors depend on the existence of a conducive investment climate and a strategic approach to FDI attraction in order to ensure the presence of a significant number of buyers. It is crucially important that the programme is implemented in a policy environment that favours private sector development and supports the creation of an enabling environment that is investment friendly and that promotes the development of domestic enterprises. In other words, what is needed is an "enabling state" rather than a "controlling state" or a "non-interventionist state";[111]

- **Fostering the emergence of a pool of qualified domestic enterprises** that are capable of supplying goods and services that meet TNCs' requirements, as well as those of the large domestic enterprises (quantity, quality and timeliness). This will depend on the policies, programmes and supporting institutions in place to assist local enterprises overcome supply-side constraints and that help strengthen their absorptive capacity so that they are able to capture linkage opportunities. In particular, supporting mechanisms may be required to promote technology upgrading, develop human capital, encourage entrepreneurship and facilitate access to finance, as described in section D.3 of this chapter;

- **Developing a selection mechanism to link TNCs, large domestic enterprises and local SMEs**. It is key to ensure that only enterprises meeting defined criteria are selected and that the TNCs and large enterprises are involved in the selection process.

Box III.8 provides a roadmap for the establishment of a Belarusian linkages programme. As already introduced in section D.2 of this chapter, Belarus should identify the pilot sectors/activities to start the linkages programme based on their propensity for backward linkages. In particular, Belarus should consider what opportunities are opened by the privatization programme to select and target strategic investors in activities that could favour the integration of the local SMEs and large companies in the TNCs' international value chain. In this respect, Belarus should consider an innovative privatization programme whereby selected vertically integrated SOEs in linkage-prone sectors (section D.2) are unbundled and strategic foreign investors are targeted to take over the core business so as to capitalize on their enhanced access to international markets, innovative production techniques and technology.

At the same time, the downstream supplier activities of the SOE should be privatized to a number of domestic companies and their integration into the value chain of the strategic investor supported by the government, including by accelerating the pro-competitiveness reforms mentioned throughout this strategy (sections D.1 to D.4) for the companies involved in the project. The pilot programme's results would be monitored and evaluated before extending it to other activities or entire sectors.

---

[111] Belarus Investment Forum, 18 November 2008, London. http://www.unctad.org/Templates/webflyer.asp?docid=10802&intItemID=3549&lang=1

Box III.8. Roadmap for a Belarusian linkages programme

Phase 1: Improve the business environment for linkages

a)   Identify and review existing and relevant policies, strategies and programmes including legal and institutional frameworks, existing matchmaking and information programmes for large companies and TNCs, incentive schemes and policies to support SMEs and FDI;

b)   Formulate recommendations on policy improvements and incentives;

c)   Publish the recommendations, secure commitment on implementing them and use the results in attracting FDI.

Phase 2: Design the linkages programme

a)   Define economic and social objectives consistent with current national development and FDI strategies;

b)   Identify potential sectors and subsectors that would benefit from a linkages programme. Define the selection criteria (with (a) in mind), for example: national strategic priorities; number of SMEs and large local companies in sector/subsector; match between local capabilities and TNCs'/large companies' input requirements; international production systems in sector/subsector; technology content; scope for moving up the value added chain; FDI inflows; level of unemployment in sector/subsector; and availability of expertise to support SMEs in sector/subsector;

c)   Select a sector/subsector for a pilot linkage programme;

d)   Develop a database of TNCs, large companies and local suppliers in the pilot sector/ subsector;

e)   Define a methodology (e.g. size of company, production capabilities) for selecting enterprises to participate;

f)   Establish a linkage programme coordination committee with key stakeholders (e.g. FDI promotion agency, SME development agency, representatives of the business community);

g)   Plan and budget for different stages of the programme (from pilot to rolling out to other sectors/subsectors) including identifying funding;

h)   Consult with relevant stakeholders to secure high-level support;

i)   Communicate objectives of the programme to relevant stakeholders;

j)   Design a monitoring mechanism to measure performance (suggested indicators: number and value of contracts, number of new SMEs in local supply chains, etc.);

k)   Design an action plan to implement the programme.

Phase 3: Implement pilot linkages programme

a)   Assess the supply chains of TNCs and large domestic companies in the selected sector/ subsector including requirements/obstacles;

b)   Identify and prioritize the specific needs of the participating suppliers;

c)   Contact selected enterprises and outline the benefits of participating in the pilot programme;

d)   Secure funding;

e)   Conduct a strategic audit (e.g. review of finances, SWOT (strengths, weaknesses, opportunities, threats) analysis, compliance with technical standards) of each participating enterprise;

f)   Jointly define a development plan (e.g. recommendations on market strategy, targeted support to improve suppliers' competencies, access to finance) with each participating enterprise;

g)   Prepare a marketing and communications package for potential foreign investors and large domestic enterprises;

h)   Market the pilot sector to both existing and potential TNCs and local enterprises that may be interested in developing partnerships with the selected local suppliers (e.g. matchmaking events);

i)   Compile feedback from interactions with foreign companies and large domestic enterprises;

j)   Measure the results from the pilot programme (quarterly and annually) including enterprise surveys;

k)   Evaluate the results and incorporate lessons learned into the framework for a wider linkages programme;

l)   Select a second sector to start an extended linkage programme.

Phase 4: Extend the linkages programme to other sectors

a)   Incorporate the results and recommendations from the pilot project into the overall linkages programme;

b)   Repeat the action steps described in phase 3 for new sectors/subsectors to be included in the linkages programme;

c)   Conduct an in-depth assessment of the outputs and outcomes (after 3–5 years operation);

d)   Communicate the results of the in-depth assessment to key stakeholders and the public to build support for FDI as a positive contribution to SME development and wider economic development;

e)   Monitor the implementation of the action plans and incorporate the results into the overall linkage programme;

f)   Disseminate information on best practice.

Source: UNCTAD (2006a) and OECD (2007).

UNCTAD stands ready to provide technical assistance in the establishment of the linkages programme for Belarus. Such a programme has been successfully implemented in other countries. For example, the UNCTAD–GTZ linkages project in Brazil aims to promote the efficiency of Brazil's domestic enterprise sector through the creation and deepening of fair and sustainable business linkages between foreign affiliates and Brazilian SMEs. Since its inception in 2005, it has enlisted 20 TNCs. One hundred and eighty SMEs have directly benefited from the project's upgrading.

CHAPTER **IV**

CONCLUSIONS AND RECOMMENDATIONS

Belarus has a lot to offer investors – a sizeable local market, privileged geographical location, developed transport infrastructure, skilled labour force and strong commitment to improving the investment climate. Entrepreneurs, domestic and foreign alike agree that the government's reforms since 2007 have clearly reduced the regulatory and administrative burden on business. The streamlining of business regulation processes, the abolishment of the Golden Share Rule, the simplification of the tax system for small and medium enterprises and the new incentives schemes to attract investment to the high technology sectors and the least developed areas of the country are illustrative of the scope of the reforms.

Nevertheless, private investment, both domestic and foreign, is still low compared to most other CIS countries. As mentioned in chapter I, the Belarusian economy is facing a number of challenges made more severe by the current global economic and financial crisis. In this context, the government's commitment to reform is an important factor in delivering much needed improvements. Fostering FDI attraction and the rejuvenation of the local public and private sector, including through FDI, requires removing remaining inhibiting factors such as the excessive regulation of business activity, the inadequacy of the competition regime and the persistence of heavy wage and price controls. It will also require effective and targeted consultation, coordination and implementation so that the recent and future reforms can trickle down to the middle to lower ranks of the bureaucracy as well as to regional and local administrations, where key bottlenecks and a predominantly planned economy attitude persist.

Following the request by the Belarusian authorities, this review prepared by UNCTAD outlines the key elements of a strategy to attract increased flows of FDI to Belarus and support SME development through FDI. The strategy can be articulated around four sets of measures aimed at: (1) improving the FDI-specific regulations; (2) enhancing the general investment climate; (3) removing obstacles to SME development; and (4) adopting targeted policy interventions to foster the developmental role of FDI for the SME sector. The main recommendations of the strategic approach outlined in this report are summarized below.

1. Improving the FDI-specific regulations

The legal framework for FDI in Belarus is open and remaining restrictions are few and relatively standard. However, there is scope for arbitrary refusals and non-transparent outcomes in the decision-making process and the treatment and protection of investors under the foreign investment law, which has fallen behind internationally accepted standards and Belarus' own BITs. Improvement to the FDI-specific regulations would thus require:

Harmonizing investors' treatment and protection with international standards. This can be achieved by introducing in the investment code protection provisions with respect to fair and equitable treatment and listing the conditions under which the standard "not less favourable" treatment of foreign investors does not apply; introducing the conditions for expropriation to be considered lawful; guaranteeing the full range of funds transfer in accordance with the BITs provisions; and providing access to domestic and international dispute resolution mechanisms for foreign investors.

Harmonizing regional and national investment legislation. The investment legislation at all levels of government should be harmonized with a view to ensuring consistency and avoiding unnecessary duplications in the state registration and other permitting processes. The conditions for refusal of an investment project should be detailed by the legislation so as to restrict the flexibility of local civil servants to assess the extent to which a project is valuable for the country on a case-by-case basis.

Strengthening the investment facilitation infrastructure. The consistent application of investment-related laws and regulations across the country is not satisfactory and administrative capacity and expertise can differ widely from region to region. Attitudes towards private investors may vary as well. In such circumstances, the central government should ensure that laws and regulations are applied consistently. In this respect, the new IPA should be assigned new functions, including troubleshooting between investors and the regions in the emergence of roadblocks to investment at the local level; providing assistance to the regions in the performance of their investment facilitation role, so as to enable all regions to attain the minimum required service standards; and monitoring and benchmarking the performance of the different regions in investment facilitation with a view to helping them improve their administrative processes when dealing with investors and fostering positive competition among them.

2. Enhancing the general investment climate

Improving the investment climate in areas such as taxation, competition and land is a necessary precondition not only to attract FDI but also to foster the development of a competitive Belarusian private sector that can efficiently compete with and supply TNCs. In this respect, the key areas for improvement as identified by this report are:

General taxation. Notwithstanding recent reforms in this area, Belarus' fiscal competitiveness is held back by a multiplicity of flat taxes based on sales, introduced at the local level, by ad hoc contributions to the various innovation funds of the public administration and by the complexity that tax reporting and payment imposes on business. This review leads to several main recommendations on re-orienting tax policy including, among others: establishing loss carry-forward for at least five years and fixing the capital depreciation rates at the highest end of the current ranges; abolishing the sales and services taxes introduced by the local authorities (and introducing appropriate revenue compensation mechanisms); replacing the "innovation funds" and other ad hoc contributions by "payments for services offered"; and replacing the monthly payments of the corporate tax and most other taxes by three payments per year.

Labour. The current wage determination system is overly rigid and does not allow investors to attract and reward managers and employees based on their skills and productivity. It is recommended that the government revise the wage classification system so as to protect the lowest paid workers by introducing different minimum wage levels for different categories of workers, while allowing entrepreneurs to freely negotiate wages above the minimum levels. The violation of trade union rights should cease as they affect the protection of workers in the country, the status of industrial relations and the image of the country vis-à-vis investors. Belarus should also consider introducing the possibility for employees to terminate fixed term contracts upon provision of sufficient notice, in accordance with international good practice.

Employment of foreigners. The procedure for hiring foreign workers is overly cumbersome and unpredictable. Belarus could benefit from attracting foreign skills through FDI, and it should make this an explicit objective of its FDI policy. Hence, the foreign workers' entry regime should be streamlined by the adoption of a one-stop approach to the expatriate entry process and the replacement of the labour market testing procedure by a predetermined list of skills shortages. Moreover, the work and residence permits should be merged and the validity of the work and residence permit should be extended according to internationally accepted practice.

Land. The new Land Code entering into force in January 2009 lays the grounds for the development of a proper real estate market. Until a sufficient number of titles are accessible through this market, however, investors will continue to find it extremely difficult to obtain land title from the state. During this transition period, it is recommended that access to land be facilitated in a number of ways, including identifying sufficient land areas to be pre-zoned and made available for commercial or industrial use; benchmarking regions against each other with respect to the support offered to investors in facilitating land access; and streamlining both the procedures for land zoning and those for land allocation by carrying out a step-by-step diagnostic of the current administrative and procedural requirements and rationalizing the coordination between the local and central authorities.

Competition. A properly level playing field among the different economic agents will be key to maximizing the benefits of FDI for the development of the local private sector and reducing potential crowding out effects from the entry of TNCs. In this respect, the competition policy and regime in Belarus need significant strengthening. In particular, this report recommends reviewing all discriminatory practices with respect to the access to inputs with a view to removing distortions where these are not strictly justified by public interest; creating an independent, professionally staffed and adequately funded National Competition Authority; and amending the competition legislation to bring it up to international standards.

Licensing. The licensing requirements have become emblematic, within Belarus, of an overly bureaucratic approach to the regulation of economic activity. The licensing regime should be further streamlined and reviewed to ensure that licences are required only for those activities that pose potential public interest concerns with respect to health, safety or consumer protection. In the process, it is important for the authorities to ensure that repealed licences are not replaced on a systematic basis by equally burdensome certification requirements. Moreover, the licence performance requirements should be streamlined so as to protect the relevant public interest without imposing unnecessary restrictions on the licensed activity, and appropriate administrative and judiciary appeal mechanisms should be introduced in case of licence withdrawal.

3.   Removing obstacles to SME development

The Belarusian SME sector is small compared to most countries in the region and other CIS countries. This report concludes that for the local SMEs to share the gains from FDI, a significant leap in competitiveness and capacity is required. FDI exposes local producers to competitive pressures and may generate short-term shocks. The government has an important role to play in mitigating these risks and maximizing the beneficial impacts for the embryonic private sector, and SMEs in particular. Removing the obstacles to SME growth is key to enhancing the capacity of local SMEs to successfully face the competition of TNCs, absorb new technology and production techniques and access new markets through FDI. Thus, the proposed strategy recommends the government to address the following SME-specific constraints:

Taxation of SMEs. The Belarusian tax system is particularly onerous for SMEs. If the Simplified System of Taxation for small enterprises helped reduce the burden of tax payment procedure for SMEs, its effectiveness in terms of offering a competitive taxation scheme remains limited as the current rates are still high and burdensome for many producers. It is thus recommended that these are reviewed against their effectiveness to achieve the intended objective, which is the development of the SME sector.

Price controls. Comprehensive price legislation bears a number of negative impacts which are more accentuated for SMEs. Apart from distorting competition, they are time- and resource-consuming and require SMEs to make recourse to specialists to avoid the fines imposed by improper implementation. Moreover, price controls discourage the creation of linkages between local SMEs and foreign companies, to which such controls do not apply. It is recommended that such price controls be removed for all but a relatively narrowly defined list of public goods.

Complexity and variability of regulations, reporting and administrative controls. The complex and excessive regulation of entrepreneurial activity is accompanied by a large number of reporting requirements and administrative controls. Given the high variability of the rules, all companies, but SMEs in particular, are exposed to very costly and time-consuming requirements that reduce their competitiveness vis-à-vis regional competitors, foster the development of the informal (shadow) economy and affect the establishment of supplier linkages. Moreover, the multitude of administrative procedures and regulations create a nourishing environment for rent-seeking behaviour in the public sector and state bureaucracy. This report joins other analysts such as the IFC in recommending the simplification of existing legislation, improved coordination among inspecting agencies, the introduction of consultative services for SMEs, the elimination of unscheduled inspections and the re-alignment of sanctions to reflect the gravity of the violations.

Education and business skills. Belarus has achieved high levels of literacy and technical expertise. However, like in most other transition economies, the education system has for long been biased towards sciences and engineering, neglecting social sciences, law and business skills. Fostering private sector development in the Belarusian economy requires a re-orientation of educational profiles. Education in business skills, especially entrepreneurship, is required at secondary schools and universities as well as vocational training and lifelong education. In order to accelerate the supply of executive talents in the medium term, the government should consider establishing a joint venture business school with competitive entry in collaboration with an internationally renowned overseas partner.

4. Adopting targeted policy interventions to foster the developmental role of FDI for the SME sector

These complementary elements of the proposed strategy aim at enabling Belarus to effectively target the type of FDI that would most contribute to its objectives and to better utilize the channels for the transmission of the gains from FDI by promoting the absorptive capacities of its SMEs and designing a comprehensive TNCs–SMEs linkages programme.

Attracting FDI to specific sectors. The establishment of a new IPA in 2009 represents an opportunity for Belarus to adopt professional and proactive investor targeting techniques both to accelerate FDI inflows and to target areas of FDI that will have the greatest developmental impact. In particular, it is recommended that the new IPA be adequately equipped to target investors in those sectors and activities most likely to generate linkages with the local economic agents. In this respect, a pilot programme is recommended that utilizes the opportunity opened by the current privatization process to select vertically integrated SOEs, unbundle them and target strategic foreign investors to the core business, while selling the downstream suppliers to domestic investors so as to promote the establishment of new value chains and the access of local SMEs to the international opportunities opened by the foreign investors.

Strengthening local absorptive capacities. International experience shows that the creation and extent of TNC–SME linkages and the internalization of spillovers from FDI are strongly influenced by the local absorptive capacity. Among the policies that the government could consider to strengthen the absorptive capacity of the local SME sector are to: open an entrepreneurship and innovation capacity-building programme such as UNCTAD's EMPRETEC programme; reduce the initial transaction costs of engaging with a research base, especially for SMEs, for instance by introducing innovation vouchers; promote relationships between a company and an academic institution in order to facilitate the transfer of knowledge, technology and skills; and establish a credit guarantee scheme to alleviate the problem of limited access to finance for SMEs in Belarus.

Designing specific linkages policies. Linkages between TNCs and SMEs are among the fastest and most effective ways of upgrading domestic enterprises, facilitating the transfer of technology, knowledge and skills, improving business and management practices, and facilitating access to finance and markets (UNCTAD, forthcoming a). In Belarus, initiatives to foster linkages are limited to matchmaking and information exchanges. A more comprehensive programme is recommended to foster linkages between local SMEs, large domestic enterprises and TNCs, based on: (a) developing a "critical mass" of buyers to ensure sufficient demand for backward linkages to take place; (b) fostering the emergence of a pool of qualified domestic enterprises that are capable of supplying goods and services that meet the requirements of TNCs and large domestic enterprises (quantity, quality and timeliness); and (c) developing a selection mechanism to link TNCs, large domestic enterprises and SMEs that ensures that only enterprises meeting defined criteria are selected and that involves TNCs and local enterprises in the selection process.

ANNEX I

BELARUS' NETWORK OF BILATERAL INVESTMENT TREATIES

Partner country / countries	Date of signature	Date of entry into force
Armenia	26 May 2001	2 October 2002
Austria	16 May 2001	1 June 2002
Bahrain	26 October 2002	...
Belgium and Luxembourg	9 April 2002	...
Bosnia and Herzegovina	29 November 2004	22 January 2006
Bulgaria	21 February 1996	11 November 1997
China	11 January 1993	14 January 1995
Croatia	26 June 2001	14 July 2005
Cuba	8 June 2000	16 August 2001
Cyprus	29 May 1998	3 September 1998
Czech Republic	14 October 1996	9 April 1998
Democratic People's Republic of Korea	24 August 2006	...
Denmark	31 March 2004	20 July 2005
Egypt	20 March 1997	18 January 2005
Finland	8 June 2006	...
France	28 October 1993	...
Germany	2 April 1993	23 September 1996
India	26 November 2002	23 November 2003
Islamic Republic of Iran	14 July 1995	23 June 2000
Israel	11 April 2000	14 August 2003
Italy	25 July 1995	12 August 1997
Jordan	20 December 2002	22 December 2005
Kuwait	10 July 2001	14 June 2003
Kyrgyzstan	30 March 1999	11 November 2001
Latvia	3 March 1998	21 December 1998
Lebanon	19 June 2001	29 December 2002
Libyan Arab Jamahiriya	1 November 2000	23 February 2002
Lithuania	5 March 1999	16 May 2002
The former Yugoslav republic of Macedonia	20 June 2001	...
Mongolia	28 May 2001	1 December 2001
Netherlands	11 April 1995	1 August 1996
Oman	10 May 2004	18 January 2005
Pakistan	22 January 1997	...
Poland	24 April 1992	18 January 1993
Qatar	17 February 2001	6 August 2004
Republic of Korea	22 April 1997	9 August 1997
Republic of Moldova	28 May 1999	19 November 1999

Romania	31 May 1995	8 January 1997
Serbia and Montenegro	6 March 1996	25 January 1997
Singapore	13 May 2000	13 January 2001
Slovakia	26 August 2005	1 September 2006
Slovenia	18 October 2006	...
Sweden	20 December 1994	1 November 1996
Switzerland	28 May 1993	13 July 1994
Syrian Arab Republic	11 March 1998	1 October 1998
Tajikistan	3 September 1998	25 August 1999
Turkey	8 August 1995	20 February 1997
Ukraine	14 December 1995	11 June 1997
United Arab Emirates	27 March 2000	16 February 2001
United Kingdom	1 March 1994	28 December 1994
United States	15 January 1994	...
Venezuela (Bolivarian Republic of)	8 December 2007	...
Viet Nam	8 July 1992	24 November 19994
Yemen	18 July 2003	...

Source: Ministry of Foreign Affairs of Belarus, 2008.

ANNEX II

UNCTAD'S TAX MODEL

Corporate taxation affects the cost of investment and its profitability, and thus the return on investment. This impact is not just a question of looking at the headline rate of tax on profits. The tax burden on the investor depends on a number of factors and their interaction, including expenses allowed, rates of capital allowances (tax depreciation), the availability of tax credits, investment allowances and tax holidays, the loss carry-forward provisions and the taxation of dividends among other things.

UNCTAD's tax modelling is a method of taking into account the most important of these variables in the fiscal regime in a manner that facilitates comparison between countries. The tax variables included in the analysis are:

- Corporate income tax;
- Rate of tax including tax holidays, if any;
- Loss carry-forward provisions;
- Capital allowances, investment allowances and investment credits;
- Tax on dividends (withholding rate on dividends paid abroad).

Financial models of project investment and financing, revenues and expenses are utilized for a hypothetical business in each industry. These are based on typical costs and revenues experienced in such businesses in a developing economy. A standard set of costs and revenues is employed so that the impact of taxation on investor return can be isolated. The business models cover a selected business within each industry.

The fiscal regime in Belarus is applied to the standard business model for each sector over 10 years commencing from the initial investment. The financial models calculate net cash flow to the investor, assuming that the company pays out all residual profits after tax (100 per cent dividend pay out) and that the investor gains the residual value of the company, which is sold after 10 years for an amount equal to its balance sheet value.

The impact of the fiscal regime is presented as the present value of tax per cent (PV tax per cent). PV tax per cent is the total of taxes and duties collected by the government over the 10 years as a percentage of the project cash flow pre-tax and post-finance where both cash flows are discounted to a present value at a rate of 10 per cent per annum. PV tax per cent thus measures how much of an investor's potential project return is taken by the government in taxes. The higher the PV tax per cent, the more the fiscal regime burdens investors and reduces the incentive to invest.

REFERENCES

Altenburg T (2000), Linkages and spillovers between transnational corporations and small and medium-sized enterprises in developing countries: opportunities and policies. TNC-SME linkages for development: issues-experiences-best practice, proceedings of the special round table on TNCs, SMEs and development, UNCTAD X. Bangkok. 15 February 2000.

Austria Telekom (2007). Press release: Telekom Austria Group acquires 70% stake in Belarusian mobile operator MDC. October. http://www.telekomaustria.com/ir/news/en/2007/1003-mdc.php.

Bearing Point. (2004). Free Zones: Performance, Lessons Learned and Implications for Zone Development. McLean, Virginia.

Belarus.by. (2008). Reform of public property and privatisation. http://www.belarus.by/en/belarus/economy/privatization.

BelCel. (2008). About the company: shareholders.

Blomström M et al. (2000). The determinants of host country spillovers from foreign direct investment. CEPR discussion paper 2350. Centre for Economic Policy Research. London.

Blomström M and Kokko A (1998). Multinational corporations and spillovers. Journal of Economic Surveys. 12 (3): 247–277.

Blomström M and Sjöholm F (1999). Technology transfer and spillovers: Does local participation with multinationals matter? European Economic Review. 43: 915–923.

Central Bank of Belarus (2006). Annual Report. Minsk.

Crespo N and Fontoura MP (2007). Determinant factors of FDI spillovers: what do we really know? World Development. 35(3).

Djankov S and Hoekman B (2000). Foreign investment and productivity growth in Czech enterprises. World Bank Economic Review. 14 (1): 49–64.

EBRD. (2006). Strategy for Belarus, as approved by the Board of Directors at its meeting on 12 December 2006. London.

Foreign Investment Consultative Council of the Council of Ministers of Belarus (2008). 10 April 2008 Session.

GET/IPM (2007). Regulatory barriers for SMEs in Belarus: the role of price regulation. http://research.by/eng/get/

GET (2007). Small and Medium Business in Belarus. Minsk.

IFC (2008). КОНТРОЛЬНАЯ И НАДЗОРНАЯ ДЕЯТЕЛЬНОСТЬ В РЕСПУБЛИКЕ БЕЛАРУСЬ

IMF (2005). Republic of Belarus: financial system stability assessment. Country Report 05/216. IMF. Washington DC.

IMF (2004). Republic of Belarus: report on observance of standards and codes – fiscal transparency module. Country Report 04/361. IMF. Washington D.C.

IPM (2008), Small and medium business in Belarus. Quarterly Review. 1Q.

IPM (2007a), Small and medium business in Belarus. Quarterly Review. 2Q.

IPM (2007b). Business in Belarus 2007.

ITUC (2008). Annual Survey of Violations of Trade Union Rights.

Javorick B (forthcoming). Can survey evidence shed light on spillovers from foreign direct investment? World Bank Research Observer.

Javorick B (2004). Does foreign direct investment increase the productivity of domestic firms? In search of spillovers through backward linkages. American Economic Review. 94 (3): 605–627.

Javorcik B and Spatareanu M (2005). Disentangling FDI spillover effects: what do firm perceptions tell us? In: Moran T et al., eds. Does Foreign Direct Investment Promote Development? Washington DC, Institute for International Economics/Centre for Global Development.

Kinoshita Y (2001). R&D and technology spillovers through FDI: innovation and absorptive capacity. CEPR discussion paper 2775. Centre for Economic Policy Research. London.

Kokko A and Blomström M (1995). Policies to encourage inflows of technology through foreign multinationals. World Development. 23 (3): 459–468.

Kokko A et al. (2001). Trade regimes and spillover effects of FDI: evidence from Uruguay. Weltwirtschaftliches Archiv. 137 (1): 124–149.

Konings J (2001). The effects of foreign direct investment on domestic firms: Evidence from firm-level panel data in emerging economies. Economics of Transition. 9 (3): 619–633.

Ministry of Foreign Affairs and Ministry of Economy. (2008). Economic and Investment Review 2008. Minsk.

MSA (2007). Statistical Yearbook of the Republic of Belarus, 2007. Minsk.

OECD (2007). How to implement FDI – SME linkage programme (draft).

OECD (2002). Foreign Direct Investment for Development: Maximising Benefits, Minimising Costs. Paris, OECD.

Robinson N, ed. (2004). Reforging the Weakest Link: Global Political Economy and Post-Soviet Change in Russia, Ukraine and Belarus. Burlington VT, Ashgate.

State Property Fund (2008). Information about Privatization of the Property of the State. Minsk.

Turkcell (2008). Press release: Turkcell signed a sale and purchase agreement to acquire 80% in BeST in Belarus. 30 July.

ÛBIG (2007). Press release: ÛBIG will invest into the construction of the modern multi-functional complex in Minsk.

UNCTAD (forthcoming a). Creating Business Linkages: A Policy Perspective.

UNCTAD (forthcoming b). Investment Policy Review of Nigeria.

UNCTAD (2008). The Principles of Investor Targeting, Third Generation Investment Promotion, Reference Manual, Module 4. United Nations publication. New York and Geneva.

UNCTAD (2006a). Business linkages programme guidelines.

UNCTAD (2006b). The Least Developed Countries Report 2006: Developing Productive Capacities. United Nations publication. New York and Geneva.

UNCTAD (2001). Promoting Linkages, World Investment Report 2001. United Nations publication. New York and Geneva.

UNDP (2005). External impact assessment of UNDP Belarus support for private sector development 1997–2004: brief report.

World Bank (2005). Belarus: Window of Opportunity to Enhance Competitiveness and Sustain Economic Growth. Washington DC, World Bank.

World Bank (2003). ICT Infrastructure and E-Readiness Assessments in the Republic of Belarus. Washington DC, World Bank.

SELECTED UNCTAD PUBLICATIONS ON TRANSNATIONAL CORPORATIONS AND FDI

A. Serial publications

World Investment Reports
http://www.unctad.org/wir

UNCTAD (2009). World Investment Report 2009: Transnational Corporations, Agricultural Production and Development. United Nations Publication. Sales No. E.09.II.D.15. New York and Geneva.

UNCTAD (2008). World Investment Report 2008: Transnational Corporations and the Infrastructure Challenge. United Nations Publication. Sales No. E.08.II.D.23. New York and Geneva.

UNCTAD (2007). World Investment Report 2007: Transnational Corporations, Extractive Industries and Development. United Nations Publication. Sales No. E.07.II.D.9. New York and Geneva.

UNCTAD (2007). World Investment Report 2007: Transnational Corporations, Extractive Industries and Development: Overview. United Nations Publication. UNCTAD/WIR/2007 (Overview). New York and Geneva.

UNCTAD (2006). World Investment Report 2006: FDI from Developing and Transition Economies: Implications for Development. United Nations Publication. Sales No. E.06.II.D.11. New York and Geneva.

UNCTAD (2006). World Investment Report 2006: FDI from Developing and Transition Economies: Implications for Development. Overview. United Nations Publication. UNCTAD/WIR/2006 (Overview). New York and Geneva.

UNCTAD (2005). World Investment Report 2005: Transnational Corporations and the Internationalization of R&D. United Nations Publication. Sales No. E.05.II.D.10. New York and Geneva.

UNCTAD (2005). World Investment Report 2005: Transnational Corporations and the Internationalization of R&D: Overview. United Nations Publication. UNCTAD/WIR/2005 (Overview). New York and Geneva.

UNCTAD (2004). World Investment Report 2004: The Shift towards Services. United Nations Publication. Sales No. E.04.II.D.36. New York and Geneva.

UNCTAD (2004). World Investment Report 2004: The Shift towards Services: Overview. United Nations Publication. UNCTAD/WIR/2004 (Overview). New York and Geneva.

UNCTAD (2003). World Investment Report 2003: FDI Policies for Development: National and International Perspectives. United Nations Publication. Sales No. E.03.II.D.8. New York and Geneva.

UNCTAD (2003). World Investment Report 2003: FDI Policies for Development: National and International Perspectives: Overview. United Nations Publication. UNCTAD/WIR/2003 (Overview). New York and Geneva.

UNCTAD (2002). World Investment Report 2002: Transnational Corporations and Export Competitiveness. United Nations Publication. Sales No. E.02.II.D.4. New York and Geneva.

UNCTAD (2002). World Investment Report 2002: Transnational Corporations and Export Competitiveness: Overview. United Nations Publication. UNCTAD/WIR/2002 (Overview). New York and Geneva.

UNCTAD (2001). World Investment Report 2001: Promoting Linkages. United Nations Publication. Sales No. E.01.II.D.12. New York and Geneva.

UNCTAD (2001). World Investment Report 2001: Promoting Linkages: Overview. United Nations Publication. UNCTAD/WIR/2001 (Overview). New York and Geneva.

UNCTAD (2000). World Investment Report 2000: Cross-border Mergers and Acquisitions and Development. United Nations Publication. Sales No. E.00.II.D.20. New York and Geneva.

UNCTAD (2000). World Investment Report 2000: Cross-border Mergers and Acquisitions and Development: Overview. United Nations Publication. UNCTAD/WIR/2000 (Overview). New York and Geneva.

UNCTAD (1999). World Investment Report 1999: Foreign Direct Investment and the Challenge of Development. United Nations Publication. Sales No. E.99.II.D.3. New York and Geneva.

UNCTAD (1999). World Investment Report 1999: Foreign Direct Investment and the Challenge of Development: Overview. United Nations Publication. UNCTAD/WIR/1999 (Overview). New York and Geneva.

UNCTAD (1998). World Investment Report 1998: Trends and Determinants. United Nations Publication. Sales No. E.98.II.D.5. New York and Geneva.

UNCTAD (1998). World Investment Report 1998: Trends and Determinants: Overview. United Nations Publication. UNCTAD/WIR/1998 (Overview). New York and Geneva.

UNCTAD (1997). World Investment Report 1997: Transnational Corporations, Market Structure and Competition Policy. United Nations Publication. Sales No. E.97.II.D. 10. New York and Geneva.

UNCTAD (1997). World Investment Report 1997: Transnational Corporations, Market Structure and Competition Policy: Overview. United Nations Publication. UNCTAD/ITE/IIT/5 (Overview). New York and Geneva.

UNCTAD (1996). World Investment Report 1996: Investment, Trade and International Policy Arrangements. United Nations Publication. Sales No. E.96.II.A. 14. New York and Geneva.

UNCTAD (1996). World Investment Report 1996: Investment, Trade and International Policy Arrangements: Overview. United Nations Publication. UNCTAD/DTCI/32 (Overview). New York and Geneva.

UNCTAD (1995). World Investment Report 1995: Transnational Corporations and Competitiveness. Sales No. E.95.II.A.9. New York and Geneva

UNCTAD (1995). World Investment Report 1995: Transnational Corporations and Competitiveness: Overview. United Nations Publication. UNCTAD/DTCI/26 (Overview). New York and Geneva.

UNCTAD (1994). World Investment Report 1994: Transnational Corporations, Employment and the Workplace. United Nations Publication. Sales No.E.94.II.A.14. New York and Geneva.

UNCTAD (1994). World Investment Report 1994: Transnational Corporations, Employment and the Workplace: An Executive Summary. United Nations Publication. UNCTAD/DTCI/10 (Overview). New York and Geneva.

UNCTAD(1993). World Investment Report 1993: Transnational Corporations and Integrated International Production. United Nations Publication. Sales No. E.93.II.A.14. New York and Geneva.

UNCTAD (1993). World Investment Report 1993: Transnational Corporations and Integrated International Production: An Executive Summary. United Nations Publication. ST/CTC/159 (Executive Summary). New York and Geneva.

DESD/TCMD (1992). World Investment Report 1992: Transnational Corporations as Engines of Growth. United Nations Publication. Sales No. E.92.II.A.24. New York.

DESD/TCMD (1992). World Investment Report 1992: Transnational Corporations as Engines of Growth: An Executive Summary. United Nations Publication. ST/CTC/143 (Executive Summary). New York.

UNCTC (1991). World Investment Report 1991: The Triad in Foreign Direct Investment. United Nations Publication. Sales No. E.9 1.II.A. 12. New York.

World Investment Directories

UNCTAD (2003). World Investment Directory: Vol. VIII: Central and Eastern Europe, 2003. United Nations publication. Sales No. E.03.II.D.12. New York and Geneva.

UNCTAD (1999). World Investment Directory, Vol. VII (Parts I and II): Asia and the Pacific, 1999. United Nations publication. Sales No. E.00.II.D.21. New York and Geneva.

UNCTAD (1996). World Investment Directory, Vol. VI: West Asia, 1996. United Nations publication. Sales No. E.97.II.A.2. New York and Geneva.

UNCTAD (1996). World Investment Directory, Vol. V: Africa, 1996. United Nations publication. Sales No. E.97.II.A.1. New York and Geneva.

UNCTAD (1994). World Investment Directory, Vol. IV: Latin America and the Caribbean, 1994. United Nations publication. Sales No. E.94.II.A.10. New York and Geneva.

UNCTAD (1992). World Investment Directory, Vol. III: Developed Countries, 1992. United Nations publication. Sales No. E.93.II.A.9. New York and Geneva.

UNCTAD (1992). World Investment Directory, Vol. II: Central and Eastern Europe, 1992. United Nations publication. Sales No. E.93.II.A.1. New York and Geneva.

UNCTAD (1992). World Investment Directory, Vol. I: Asia and the Pacific, 1992. United Nations publication. Sales No. E.92.II.A.11. New York and Geneva.

Investment Policy Reviews
http://www.unctad.org/ipr

UNCTAD (2009). Investment Policy Review of Burkina Faso. United Nations publication. UNCTAD/DIAE/ PCB/2009/04. New York and Geneva.

UNCTAD (2009). Investment Policy Review of Mauritania. United Nations publication. UNCTAD/DIAE/ PCB/2008/05. New York and Geneva.

UNCTAD (2009). Investment Policy Review of Nigeria. United Nations publication. UNCTAD/DIAE/ PCB/2008/01. New York and Geneva.

UNCTAD (2009). Investment Policy Review of the Dominican Republic. United Nations publication. UNCTAD/ITE/IPC/2007/09. New York and Geneva.

UNCTAD (2008). Investment Policy Review of Viet Nam. United Nations publication. UNCTAD/ITE/ IPC/2007/10. New York and Geneva.

UNCTAD (2008). Investment Policy Review of Morocco. United Nations publication. UNCTAD/ITE/ IPC/2006/15. New York and Geneva.

UNCTAD (2007). Investment Policy Review of Zambia. United Nations publication. UNCTAD/ITE/ IPC/2006/14. New York and Geneva.

UNCTAD (2007). Report on the Implementation of the Investment Policy Review of Uganda. United Nations publication. UNCTAD/ITE/IPC/2006/15. New York and Geneva.

UNCTAD (2006). Investment Policy Review of Rwanda. United Nations publication. UNCTAD/ITE/IPC/2006/11. New York and Geneva.

UNCTAD (2006). Investment Policy Review of Colombia. United Nations publication. UNCTAD/ITE/IPC/2005/11. New York and Geneva.

UNCTAD (2005). Report on the Implementation of the Investment Policy Review of Egypt. United Nations publication. UNCTAD/ITE/IPC/2005/7. New York and Geneva.

UNCTAD (2005). Investment Policy Review of Kenya. United Nations publication. UNCTAD/ITE/IPC/2005/8. New York and Geneva.

UNCTAD (2005). Investment Policy Review of Benin. United Nations publication. UNCTAD/ITE/IPC/2004/4. New York and Geneva.

UNCTAD (2004). Investment Policy Review of Algeria. United Nations publication. UNCTAD/ITE/IPC/2003/9. New York and Geneva.

UNCTAD (2003). Investment Policy Review of Sri Lanka. United Nations publication. UNCTAD/ITE/IPC/2003/8. New York and Geneva.

UNCTAD (2003). Investment Policy Review of Lesotho. United Nations publication. Sales No. E.03.II.D.18. New York and Geneva.

UNCTAD (2003). Investment Policy Review of Nepal. United Nations publication. Sales No.E.03.II.D.17. New York and Geneva.

UNCTAD (2002). Investment Policy Review of Ghana United Nations publication. Sales No. E.02.II.D.20. New York and Geneva.

UNCTAD (2003). Investment Policy Review of Botswana. United Nations publication. Sales No. E.03.II.D.1. New York and Geneva.

UNCTAD (2002). Investment Policy Review of the United Republic of Tanzania. United Nations publication. Sales No. E.02.II.D.6. New York and Geneva.

UNCTAD (2001). Investment and Innovation Policy Review of Ethiopia. United Nations publication. Sales No. E.01.II.D.5. New York and Geneva.

UNCTAD (2001). Investment Policy Review of Ecuador. United Nations publication. Sales No. E.01.II.D.31. New York and Geneva.

UNCTAD (2000). Investment Policy Review of Mauritius. United Nations publication. Sales No. E.00.II.D.11. New York and Geneva.

UNCTAD (2000). Investment Policy Review of Peru. United Nations publication. Sales No. E.00.II.D.7. New York and Geneva.

UNCTAD (1999). Investment Policy Review of Uganda. United Nations publication. Sales No. E.99.II.D.24. New York and Geneva.

UNCTAD (1999). Investment Policy Review of Uzbekistan. United Nations publication. UNCTAD/ITE/IIP/Misc.13. New York and Geneva.

UNCTAD (1999). Investment Policy Review of Egypt. United Nations publication. Sales No. E.99.II.D.20. New York and Geneva.

Blue Books on Best Practice in Investment Promotion and Facilitation

UNCTAD (2009). Blue Book on Best Practice in Investment Promotion and Facilitation: Nigeria. New York and Geneva.

UNCTAD (2007). Blue Book on Best Practice in Investment Promotion and Facilitation: Zambia. New York and Geneva.

UNCTAD (2005). Blue Book on Best Practice in Investment Promotion and Facilitation: Kenya. New York and Geneva.

UNCTAD (2005). Blue Book on Best Practice in Investment Promotion and Facilitation: United Republic of Tanzania. New York and Geneva.

UNCTAD (2005). Blue Book on Best Practice in Investment Promotion and Facilitation: Uganda. New York and Geneva.

UNCTAD (2004). Blue Book on Best Practice in Investment Promotion and Facilitation: Cambodia. New York and Geneva.

UNCTAD (2004). Blue Book on Best Practice in Investment Promotion and Facilitation: Lao People's Democratic Republic. New York and Geneva.

Investment Guides
http://www.unctad.org/investmentguides

UNCTAD (2006). An Investment Guide to Rwanda: Opportunities and Conditions. United Nations publication. UNCTAD/ITE/IIA/2006/3. New York and Geneva.

UNCTAD (2006). An Investment Guide to Mali: Opportunities and Conditions. United Nations publication. UNCTAD/ITE/IIA/2006/2. New York and Geneva.

UNCTAD and ICC (2005). An Investment Guide to East Africa. United Nations publication. UNCTAD/IIA/2005/4. New York and Geneva.

UNCTAD and ICC (2005). An Investment Guide to the United Republic of Tanzania. United Nations publication. UNCTAD/IIA/2005/3. New York and Geneva.

UNCTAD and ICC (2005). An Investment Guide to Kenya. United Nations publication. UNCTAD/IIA/2005/2. New York and Geneva.

UNCTAD and ICC (2004). An Investment Guide to Mauritania. United Nations publication. UNCTAD/IIA/2004/4. New York and Geneva.

UNCTAD and ICC (2003). An Investment Guide to Cambodia. United Nations publication. UNCTAD/IIA/2003/6. New York and Geneva.

UNCTAD and ICC (2003). An Investment Guide to Nepal. United Nations publication. UNCTAD/IIA/2003/2. New York and Geneva.

UNCTAD and ICC (2002). An Investment Guide to Mozambique. United Nations publication. UNCTAD/IIA/4. New York and Geneva.

UNCTAD and ICC (2001). An Investment Guide to Uganda. United Nations publication. UNCTAD/ITE/IIT/Misc.30. Updated in 2004: new document symbol UNCTAD/ITE/IIA/2004/3. New York and Geneva.

UNCTAD and ICC (2001). An Investment Guide to Mali. United Nations publication. UNCTAD/ITE/IIT/

Misc.24. Updated in 2004: new document symbol UNCTAD/ITE/IIA/2004/1. New York and Geneva.

UNCTAD and ICC. An Investment Guide to Ethiopia. United Nations publication. UNCTAD/ITE/IIT/Misc.19. Updated in 2004: new document symbol UNCTAD/ITE/IIA/2004/2. New York and Geneva.

 UNCTAD and ICC (2000). An Investment Guide to Bangladesh. United Nations publication. UNCTAD/ITE/IIT/Misc.29. New York and Geneva.

Issues in International Investment Agreements
http://www.unctad.org/iia

UNCTAD (2006). Bilateral Investment Treaties 1995–2006: Trends in Investment Rulemaking United Nations publication. New York and Geneva.

UNCTAD (2006). Investment Provisions in Economic Integration Agreements. United Nations publication. New York and Geneva.

UNCTAD (2003). Glossary of Key Concepts Used in IIAs; UNCTAD Series on Issues in International Investment Agreements. United Nations publication. New York and Geneva.

UNCTAD (2003). Incentives: UNCTAD Series on Issues in International Investment Agreements. United Nations publication. Sales No. E.04.II.D.6. New York and Geneva.

UNCTAD (2003). Transparency: UNCTAD Series on Issues in International Investment Agreements. United Nations publication. Sales No. E.03.II.D.7. New York and Geneva.

UNCTAD (2003). Dispute Settlement: Investor–State: UNCTAD Series on Issues in International Investment Agreements. United Nations publication. Sales No. E.03.II.D.5. New York and Geneva.

UNCTAD (2003). Dispute Settlement: State–State: UNCTAD Series on Issues in International Investment Agreements. United Nations publication. Sales No. E.03.II.D.6. New York and Geneva.

UNCTAD (2001). Transfer of Technology: UNCTAD Series on Issues on International Investment Agreements. United Nations publication. Sales No. E.01.II.D.33. New York and Geneva.

UNCTAD (2001). Illicit Payments: UNCTAD Series on Issues on International Investment Agreements. United Nations publication. Sales No. E.01.II.D.20. New York and Geneva.

UNCTAD (2001). Home Country Measures: UNCTAD Series on Issues on International Investment Agreements. United Nations publication. Sales No. E.01.II.D.19. New York and Geneva.

UNCTAD (2001). Host Country Operational Measures: UNCTAD Series on Issues on International Investment Agreements. United Nations publication. Sales No. E.01.II.D.18. New York and Geneva.

UNCTAD (2001). Social Responsibility: UNCTAD Series on Issues on International Investment Agreements. United Nations publication. Sales No. E.01.II.D.4. New York and Geneva.

UNCTAD (2001). Environment: UNCTAD Series on Issues on International Investment Agreements. United Nations publication. Sales No. E.01.II.D.3. New York and Geneva.

UNCTAD (2000). Transfer of Funds: UNCTAD Series on Issues on International Investment Agreements. United Nations publication. Sales No. E.00.II.D.38. $10. New York and Geneva.

UNCTAD (2000). Flexibility for Development: UNCTAD Series on Issues on International Investment Agreements. United Nations publication. Sales No. E.00.II.D.6. New York and Geneva.

UNCTAD (2000). Employment: UNCTAD Series on Issues on International Investment Agreements. United

Nations publication. Sales No. E.00.II.D.15. New York and Geneva.

UNCTAD (2000). Taxation: UNCTAD Series on Issues on International Investment Agreements. United Nations publication. Sales No. E.00.II.D.5. New York and Geneva.

UNCTAD (2000). Taking of Property: UNCTAD Series on Issues on International Investment Agreements. Sales No. E.00.II.D.4. New York and Geneva.

UNCTAD (1999). Trends in International investment Agreements: An Overview: UNCTAD Series on Issues on International Investment Agreements. United Nations publication. Sales No. E.99.II.D.23. New York and Geneva.

UNCTAD (1999). Lessons from the MAI: UNCTAD Series on Issues on International Investment Agreements. United Nations publication. Sales No. E.99.II.D.26. New York and Geneva.

UNCTAD (1999). National Treatment: UNCTAD Series on Issues in International Investment Agreements. United Nations publication. Sales No. E.99.II.D. 16. New York and Geneva.

UNCTAD (1999). Fair and Equitable Treatment: UNCTAD Series on Issues in International Investment Agreements. United Nations publication. Sales No. E.99.II.D.15. New York and Geneva.

UNCTAD (1999). Investment-Related Trade Measures: UNCTAD Series on Issues in International Investment Agreements. United Nations publication. Sales No. E.99.II.D.12. New York and Geneva.

UNCTAD (1999). Most-Favoured-Nation Treatment: UNCTAD Series on Issues in International Investment Agreements. United Nations publication. Sales No. E.99.II.D.11. New York and Geneva.

UNCTAD (1999). Admission and Establishment: UNCTAD Series on Issues in International Investment Agreements. United Nations publication. Sales No. E.99.II.D.10. New York and Geneva.

UNCTAD (1999). Scope and Definition: UNCTAD Series on Issues in International Investment Agreements. United Nations publication. Sales No. E.99.II.D.9. New York and Geneva.

UNCTAD (1999). Transfer Pricing: UNCTAD Series on Issues in International Investment Agreements. United Nations publication, Sales No. E.99.II.D.8. New York and Geneva.

UNCTAD (1999). Foreign Direct Investment and Development: UNCTAD Series on Issues in International Investment Agreements. United Nations publication. Sales No. E.98.II.D.15A12. New York and Geneva.

International Investment Instruments

UNCTAD. UNCTAD's work programme on international investment agreements: from UNCTAD IX to UNCTAD X. UNCTAD/ITE/IIT/Misc.26. Geneva.

UNCTAD (2002). Progress report: work undertaken within UNCTAD's work programme on International Investment Agreements between the 10th Conference of UNCTAD, Bangkok, February 2000, and July 2002. UNCTAD/ITE/Misc.58. Geneva.

UNCTAD (1998). Bilateral Investment Treaties in the Mid-1990s. United Nations publication. Sales No. E.98. II.D.8. New York and Geneva.

UNCTAD (2000). Bilateral Investment Treaties: 1959–1999. United Nations publication. Sales No. E.92. II.A.16. New York and Geneva.

UNCTAD (1996–2003). International Investment Instruments: A Compendium. United Nations publication, 12 volumes. Vol. I: Sales No. E.96.A.II.A.9. Vol. II: Sales No. E.96.II.A.10. Vol. III: Sales No. E.96.II.A.11. Vol. IV:

Sales No. E.00.II.D.13. Vol. V: Sales No. E.00.II.A.14. Vol. VI: Sales No. E.01.II.D.34. Vol. VII: Sales No. E.02. II.D.14. Vol. VIII: Sales No. E.02.II.D.15. Vol. IX: Sales No. E.02.II.D.16. Vol. X: Sales No. E.02.II.D.21. Vol. XI: Sales No. E.04.II.D.9. Vol. XII: Sales No. E.04.II.D.10. New York and Geneva

UNCTC and ICC (1992). Bilateral Investment Treaties: A Joint Publication by the United Nations Centre on Transnational Corporations and the International Chamber of Commerce. United Nations publication. Sales No. E.92.II.A. 16. New York.

UNCTC (1990). The New Code Environment: Current Studies, Series A, No. 16. United Nations publication. Sales No. E.90.II.A.7. Out of print. Available on microfiche. New York.

UNCTC (1990). Key Concepts in International Investment Arrangements and Their Relevance to Negotiations on International Transactions in Services: Current Studies, Series A, No. 13. United Nations publication. Sales No. E.90.II.A.3. New York.

UNCTC (1988). Bilateral Investment Treaties. United Nations publication. Sales No. E.88.II.A. 1. New York.

UNCTC (1986). The United Nations Code of Conduct on Transnational Corporations: Current Studies, Series A, No. 4. United Nations publication. Sales No. E.86.II.A. 15. Out of print. Available on microfiche. New York.

Vagts D (1986). The Question of a Reference to International Obligations in the United Nations Code of Conduct on Transnational Corporations: A Different View: Current Studies, Series A, No. 2. United Nations Publication. Sales No. E.86.II.A.11. Out of print. Available on microfiche. New York.

Robinson P (1986). The Question of a Reference to International Law in the United Nations Code of Conduct on Transnational Corporations: Current Studies, Series A, No.1. United Nations publication. Sales No. E.86.II.A.5. New York.

UNCTC (1977). Transnational Corporations: Material Relevant to the Formulation of a Code of Conduct. United Nations publication. EX. 10/ 10 and Corr. 1. New York.

UNCTC (1976). Transnational Corporations: Issues Involved in the Formulation of a Code of Conduct. United Nations publication. Sales No. E.77.II.A.5. Out of print. Available on microfiche. New York.

ASIT Advisory Studies
http://www.unctad.org/asit

UNCTAD (2001). No. 17: The World of Investment Promotion at a Glance: A Survey of Investment Promotion Practices. United Nations publication. UNCTAD/ITE/IPC/3. New York and Geneva.

UNCTAD. No. 16: Tax Incentives and Foreign Direct Investment: A Global Survey. United Nations publication. Sales No. E.01.II.D.5. New York and Geneva.

UNCTAD. No. 15: Investment Regimes in the Arab World: Issues and Policies. United Nations publication. Sales No. E/F.00.II.D.32. New York and Geneva.

UNCTAD. No. 14: Handbook on Outward Investment Promotion Agencies and Institutions. United Nations publication. Sales No. E.99.II.D.22. New York and Geneva.

UNCTAD. No. 13: Survey of Best Practices in Investment Promotion. United Nations publication. Sales No. E.97.II.D.11. New York and Geneva.

B. Individual Studies

UNCTAD (2003). Investment and Technology Policies for Competitiveness: Review of Successful Country Experiences. United Nations publication. UNCTAD/ITE/ICP/2003/2. Geneva.

UNCTAD (2003). The Development Dimension of FDI: Policy and Rule-Making Perspectives. United Nations publication. Sales No. E.03.II.D.22. Geneva.

UNCTAD (2003). FDI and Performance Requirements: New Evidence from Selected Countries. United Nations publication. Sales No. E.03.II.D.32. Geneva.

UNCTAD (2001). Measures of the Transnationalization of Economic Activity. United Nations publication. UNCTAD/ITE/IIA/1. Sales No. E.01.II.D.2. New York and Geneva.

UNCTAD (2000). FDI Determinants and TNC Strategies: The Case of Brazil. United Nations publication. Sales No. E.00:II.D.2. Geneva.

UNCTAD (2000). The Competitiveness Challenge: Transnational Corporations and Industrial Restructuring in Developing Countries. United Nations publication. Sales No. E.00.II.D.35. Geneva.

UNCTAD (1999). Foreign Direct Investment in Africa: Performance and Potential. United Nations publication. UNCTAD/ITE/IIT/Misc.15. Geneva.

UNCTAD (1998). The Financial Crisis in Asia and Foreign Direct Investment: An Assessment. United Nations publication. Sales No. GV.E.98.0.29. Geneva.

UNCTAD (1998). Handbook on Foreign Direct Investment by Small and Medium-sized Enterprises: Lessons from Asia. United Nations publication. Sales No. E.98.II.D.4. New York and Geneva.

UNCTAD. Handbook on Foreign Direct Investment by Small and Medium-sized Enterprises: Lessons from Asia: Executive Summary and Report on the Kunming Conference. United Nations publication. UNCTAD/ITE/IIT/6 (Summary). Geneva.

UNCTAD (1997). Survey of Best Practices in Investment Promotion. United Nations publication. Sales No. E.97.II.D.11. New York and Geneva.

UNCTAD (1996). Incentives and Foreign Direct Investment: Current Studies, Series A, No. 30. United Nations publication. Sales No. E.96.II.A.6. New York and Geneva.

UNCTC (1988). Foreign Direct Investment in the People's Republic of China. United Nations publication. Sales No. E.88.II.A.3. Out of print. Available on microfiche. New York.

UNCTAD and International Organization for Migration (1996). Foreign Direct Investment, Trade, Aid and Migration Current Studies, Series A, No. 29. United Nations publication. Sales No. E.96M.A.8. Geneva.

UNCTAD (1993). Explaining and Forecasting Regional Flows of Foreign Direct Investment: Current Studies, Series A, No. 26. United Nations publication. Sales No. E.94.II.A.5. New York.

UNCTAD (1993). Small and Medium-sized Transnational Corporations: Role, Impact and Policy Implications. United Nations publication. Sales No. E.93.II.A. 15. New York and Geneva.

UNCTAD (1994). Small and Medium-sized Transnational Corporations: Executive Summary and Report of the Osaka Conference. United Nations publication. Geneva.

DESD/TCMD (1993). From the Common Market to EC 92: Regional Economic Integration in the European Community and Transnational Corporations. United Nations publication. Sales No. E.93.II.A.2. New York.

DESD/TCMD (1993). Debt–Equity Swaps and Development. United Nations publication. Sales No. E.93.II. A.7. New York.

DESD/TCMD (1993). Transnational Corporations from Developing Countries: Impact on Their Home Countries. United Nations publication. Sales No. E.93.II.A.8. New York.

DESD/TCMD (1993). Foreign Investment and Trade Linkages in Developing Countries. United Nations publication. Sales No. E.93.II.A. 12. Out of print. New York.

UNCTC (1992). Foreign Direct Investment and Industrial Restructuring in Mexico: Current Studies, Series A, No. 18. Sales No. E.92.II.A.9. New York.

UNCTC (1992). The Determinants of Foreign Direct Investment: A Survey of the Evidence. United Nations publication. Sales No. E.92.II.A.2. New York.

UNCTC and UNCTAD (1991). The Impact of Trade-Related Investment Measures on Trade and Development. United Nations publication. Sales No. E.91 II.A. 19. Geneva and New York.

UNCTC (1991). The Challenge of Free Economic Zones in Central and Eastern Europe: International Perspective. United Nations publication. Sales No. E.90.II.A.27. New York.

UNCTC (1990). The Role of Free Economic Zones in the USSR and Eastern Europe: Current Studies, Series A, No. 14. United Nations publication. Sales No. E.90.II.A.5. New York.

UNCTC (1990). Foreign Direct Investment, Debt and Home Country Policies: Current Studies, Series A, No. 20. United Nations publication. Sales No. E.90.II.A. 16. New York.

UNCTC (1990). News Issues in the Uruguay Round of Multilateral Trade Negotiations: Current Studies, Series A, No. 19. United Nations publication. Sales No. E.90.II.A. 15. New York.

UNCTC (1990). Regional Economic Integration and Transnational Corporations in the 1990s: Europe 1992, North America, and Developing Countries: Current Studies, Series A, No. 15. United Nations publication. Sales No. E.90.II.A. 14. New York.

UNCTC (1989). Transnational Corporations and International Economic Relations: Recent Developments and Selected Issues: Current Studies, Series A, No. 11. United Nations publication. Sales No. E.89.II.A.15. Out of print. Available on microfiche. New York.

UNCTC (1989). The Process of Transnationalization and Transnational Mergers. Current Studies, Series A, No. 8. United Nations publication. Sales No. E.89.II.A.4. Out of print. Available on microfiche. New York.

UNCTC and ILO (1988). Economic and Social Effects of Multinational Enterprises in Export Processing Zones. United Nations publication. ISBN: 92-2106194-9. S1727.50. Geneva.

UNCTC (1982). Measures Strengthening the Negotiating Capacity of Governments in Their Relations with Transnational Corporations: Regional Integration cum/versus Corporate Integration: A Technical Paper. United Nations publication. Sales No. E..82.II.A.6. Out of print. Available on microfiche. New York.

C. Journals

Transnational Corporations Journal (formerly The CTC Reporter). Published three times a year. http://www.unctad.org/tnc

READERSHIP SURVEY
Investment Policy Review of Belarus

In order to improve the quality and relevance of the work of the UNCTAD Division on Investment, Technology and Enterprise Development, it would be useful to receive the views of readers on this and other similar publications. It would therefore be greatly appreciated if you could complete the following questionnaire and return it to:

Readership Survey
UNCTAD, Division on Investment, Technology and Enterprise Development
Palais des Nations
Room E-10074
CH-1211 Geneva 10
Switzerland
Or by Fax to: 41-22-9170197

> This questionnaire is also available to be filled out on line at:
> **www.unctad.org/ipr**

1. Name and professional address of respondent (optional):

2. Which of the following best describes your area of work?

    Government ○   Public enterprise ○

    Private enterprise institution ○   Academic or research ○

    International organization ○   Media ○

    Not-for-profit organization ○   (Other (specify ○

3. In which country do you work?

4. What is your assessment of the contents of this publication?

    Excellent ○   Adequate ○

    Good ○   Poor ○

5. How useful is this publication to your work?

    Very useful ○   Of some use ○   Irrelevant ○

6. Please indicate the three things you liked best about this publication and are useful to your work:

7. Please indicate the three things you liked least about this publication:

_____

_____

_____

8. If you have read more than the present publication of the UNCTAD Division on Investment, Enterprise Development and Technology, what is your overall assessment of them?

Consistently good ◯   Usually good, but with some exceptions ◯

Generally mediocre ◯   Poor ◯

9. On the average, how useful are these publications to you in your work?

Irrelevant ◯   Of some use ◯   Very useful ◯

10. Are you a regular recipient of Transnational Corporations (formerly The CTC Reporter), the Division's tri-annual refereed journal?

No ◯   Yes ◯

If not, please check here if you would like to receive a sample copy sent to the name and address you have given above. Other titles you would like to receive instead (see list of publications).

_____

_____

11. How or where did you get this publication:

I bought it ◯   In a seminar/workshop ◯

I requested a courtesy copy ◯   Direct mailing ◯

Other ◯

12. Would you like to receive information on the work of UNCTAD in the area of Investment Technology and Enterprise Development through e-mail ? If yes, please write your e-mail address below:

United Nations publications may be obtained from bookstores and distributors throughout the world. Please consult your bookstore or write to:

For Africa and Europe:
Sales Section
United Nations Office at Geneva
Palais des Nations
CH-1211 Geneva 10
Switzerland
Tel: 41 22 917 1234
Fax: 41 22 917 0123
E-mail: unpubli@unog.ch

For Asia and the Pacific, the Caribbean, Latin America and North America:
Sales Section
Room DC2-0853
United Nations Secretariat
New York, NY 10017
United States
Tel: 1 212 963 8302 or 1 800 253 9646
Fax: 1 212 963 3489
E-mail: publications@un.org
All prices are quoted in United States dollars.

For further information on the work of the Division on Investment and Enterprise, UNCTAD, please address inquiries to:
United Nations Conference on Trade and Development
Division on Investment and Enterprise
Palais des Nations, Room E-10054
CH-1211 Geneva 10, Switzerland
Telephone: 41 22 917 5534
Fax: 41 22 917 0498
http://www.unctad.org